Gender and the London Theatre
1880–1920

Gender and the London Theatre 1880–1920

MARGARET D. STETZ

Published by the RIVENDALE PRESS
in association with BRYN MAWR COLLEGE LIBRARY

2004

Published by

RIVENDALE PRESS
P. O. Box 85
High Wycombe
Buckinghamshire HP14 4WZ
United Kingdom
www.rivendalepress.com

in association with

BRYN MAWR COLLEGE LIBRARY
Bryn Mawr College
101 North Merion Avenue
Bryn Mawr, Pennsylvania 19010
United States
www.brynmawr.edu

This book records the exhibition, "Gender and the London Theatre, 1880–1920," held in the Class of 1912 Rare Book Room in the Mariam Coffin Canaday Library, Bryn Mawr College, Bryn Mawr, Pennsylvania, from 28 September to 21 December 2003.

ISBN 1 904201 00 8

Printed and Bound by ANTONY ROWE LTD., CHIPPENHAM, ENGLAND
Designed by MARK SAMUELS LASNER

Contents

List of Plates

I. Mabel Dearmer, Poster for Ibsen's *Brand,* Act IV; *School for Scandal,* Quarrel Scene, &c, Dramatically Rendered by Mrs. Percy Dearmer, Princes Hall, Piccadilly, color lithograph, [ca. 1895].

II. Albert Morrow, Poster for *The New Woman* by Sydney Grundy, color lithograph, [1897].

III. Aubrey Beardsley, Poster for *A Comedy of Sighs* by John Todhunter and *The Land of Heart's Desire* by W. B. Yeats, color lithograph, 1894.

IV. *Studio Scene from "Trilby,"* toy theatre, color lithograph, 1896.

V. John Hassall, Poster for *The Wild Rabbit* by George Arliss, color lithograph, [1899].

VI. G. F. [George Frederick] Scotson-Clark, *Marie Lloyd,* in *The "Halls,"* [1899].

VII. *Evelyn Millard,* heliochrome reproduction of photograph by Alfred Ellis, in Boyle Lawrence, ed., *Celebrities of the Stage,* [1899–1900].

VIII. Pamela Colman Smith, Poster for *Shakespeare's Heroines Calendar 1899,* color lithograph, [1898].

Foreword

THIS VOLUME is the product of an exhibition, "Gender and the London Theatre, 1880–1920," presented at the Bryn Mawr College Library during the fall of 2003. The exhibition had its origins two years earlier in my conversation with the curators, Dr. Margaret D. Stetz and Mark Samuels Lasner, about the possibility of a show at Bryn Mawr that would draw upon their extensive knowledge of the Victorian world, the former's deep understanding of Victorian women writers and of gender issues, and the latter's extraordinary collection of Victorian books, documents, and graphics. "Gender and the London Theatre" was the happy result.

Between that conversation and the opening of the exhibition, both the Samuels Lasner and Bryn Mawr collections added promising new items for display, including two key pieces: Pamela Colman Smith's poster for *Shakespeare's Heroines Calendar 1899* (Samuels Lasner), and the 1907 postcard of actress Maud Allan in costume for the title role in Oscar Wilde's *Salome* (Bryn Mawr).

The exhibition opened 28 September 2003 with Dr. Stetz's lecture on the ways in which late-Victorian women experienced the theatre as performers, audience members, authors, and readers. That lecture has been adapted here as the introductory essay, "Playbooks: The Stage on the Page at the Turn of the Century," and the text that she wrote for the exhibition labels has become the basis for the remainder of this volume.

On 22 November we devoted a day-long symposium to intensive discussion of women and gender issues on the London stage as an accompaniment to the show. At that symposium, David C. Rose, editor of *The Oscholars: Journal of Wilde Studies,* looked at how the portrayal of gender evolved on stage over the course of the late nineteenth and early twentieth centuries. Dr. Lois Potter, Ned B. Allen Professor of English at the University of Delaware, explored the career of feminist actress and writer Elizabeth Robins. In between, we experienced at firsthand how male playwrights were coming to terms with the British "New Woman" through a delightful performance of J.M. Barrie's one-act play, *The Twelve-Pound Look,* first produced in 1910, and recreated by a group of current and former Bryn Mawr and Haverford College students.

The success of the exhibition was the result of hard work by many talented people. Most of all, of course, thanks are due to the curators, Dr. Stetz and Mr. Samuels Lasner. "Gender and the London Theatre" is only the most recent in the influential string of exhibitions, conferences, and publications that have resulted from their remarkable collaboration. Thanks also go to Jane Tippett, a University of Delaware student who worked with the curators in selecting and researching items for display; Barbara Ward Grubb and Marianne Hansen, of the Bryn Mawr Special Collections staff, who handled so brilliantly the installation of the exhibition;

Raymond Nichols, Professor of Art/Visual Communications at the University of Delaware, for help with the illustrations; and Mark Garvin, who photographed the posters for this book. I am also grateful to the University of Delaware Library and in particular to Timothy D. Murray, Head of Special Collections, for the loan of a rare George Bernard Shaw rehearsal copy. Finally, I wish to thank the Friends of the Bryn Mawr College Library, whose financial support made both the exhibition and this book possible, and especially a member of the Friends board, Steven Rothman, who introduced Margaret Stetz and Mark Samuels Lasner to Bryn Mawr.

Eric L. Pumroy
Director of Library Collections
and Seymour Adelman Head of Special Collections
Bryn Mawr College

Playbooks: The Stage on the Page at the Turn of the Century

METAPHORICALLY, all the world may be a stage. But at the turn of the century, all of London seemed literally to be a theatre. There were theatres—whether licensed and open to the public or unlicensed and functioning as private clubs run by subscription—and professional companies in every location. They catered to a variety of tastes, income levels, and populations both indigenous and transplanted, with performances in English (modern and Elizabethan), in French, or in Yiddish. Some of their offerings were comic and some dramatic, some with music or with song and dance, and others without. To list even a few of the dozens upon dozens of major venues open in the 1890s is to chant a sort of tone poem: the Alexandra, Bedford, Britannia, Camden, Comedy, Court, Criterion, Daly's, Empire, Gaiety, Garrick, Grand, Haymarket, Kingsway, Lyceum, and on and on down through the alphabet. We might stop appropriately enough with a mention of the Lyric, for these were all names that belonged in a lyric (or perhaps an epic)—names that were tributes to royalty, to concepts of nationalism and imperial successes, to great theatrical figures of the past or to late-nineteenth-century entrepreneurs, to neighborhoods, to the Classical heritage, or to dramatic genres. Alongside the many officially recognized sites, there were also countless halls rented for a night or two, political meeting-houses occasionally turned into theatres, large sitting-rooms fitted out with rows of chairs, and back-gardens ringed with spectators, where amateur players staged their entertainments for friends and family, activists used drama for rabble-rousing or fundraising, and professional actors sometimes performed on behalf of charities.

To appreciate the range of theatrical spectacle available by the last decade of the nineteenth century, merely at theatres formally constituted as such, let us go back to the beginning of the alphabet and consider the entertainments at three of these: the Adelphi, the Avenue, and the Alhambra.

The Adelphi was immortalized in a popular phrase, "Adelphi melodramas," and there was no better place in London for audiences that wished to be brought to tears, titillated by passionate declarations of love, or rendered awestuck by eye-popping stage effects. Movie patrons today who seek out the latest computer-generated explosions in blockbuster Hollywood action pictures had their theatre-going equivalents at the turn of the century. The Adelphi offered them recreations of a thunderstorm onstage in Henry Pettitt's 1893 *A Woman's Revenge*; a working lift—that is, an elevator—descending upon and threatening to crush Marion Terry (one of the actress-sisters of Ellen Terry) in Sutton Vane's 1894 *The Cotton King*; a bomb appearing to go off and wreck the scenery in the 1894 *The Fatal Card*; and the sight of a boat in roiling waters, buffeted by fierce winds, in the 1895 *The Swordsman's Daughter*, adapted from a French hit by the team of theatre critic Clement Scott and

Brandon Thomas. (The latter was better known as author of the cross-dressing comedy, *Charley's Aunt*.) Yet the most sensational and melodramatic moment at the Adelphi happened backstage and was experienced not by playgoers, but by the newspaper-reading public: that was the 1897 murder at the Adelphi stage door of leading-man William Terriss, who was stabbed to death by an out-of-work actor gone berserk.

If the Adelphi served the needs of thrill-seekers whose tastes were otherwise conservative, and who expected happy endings in which of villains were punished and virtuous women rescued from danger, the Avenue Theatre in Northumberland Avenue became the destination of choice during the mid-Nineties for more serious, literary-minded audiences. Female actor-managers were rare. But in 1894, the novelist and actress Florence Farr proved herself as much an impresario as a performer by bringing to the Avenue the first London production of a play by W.B. Yeats, a venture financed by Annie Horniman. Yeats's *The Land of Heart's Desire* demonstrated that the Celtic Renaissance would revolutionize Irish theatre, even as it revivified Irish verse. Thanks to Florence Farr, moreover, patrons of the Avenue were privy to another important moment during the same season—the premiere of G.B. Shaw's anti-war comedy, *Arms and the Man*. Two years later, in 1896, the Avenue saw women again assume control and present challenging, progressive work. The American-born actress Elizabeth Robins and her colleague Marion Lea produced Ibsen's *Little Eyolf* there, as part of Robins's ongoing efforts to introduce the Norwegian dramatist to England and to use his plays as a sword of righteousness, with which to cut through tired stage conventions and to skewer middle-class certainties.

But if theatregoers came home from these shows at the Avenue Theatre in a sombre, thoughtful frame of mind, they returned from a night at the Alhambra in a different mood entirely—if they returned at all. Indeed, if they were gentlemen who had arrived at this music hall on their own, they often did not leave alone or retire to their own beds. Like its even more notorious neighbor in Leicester Square, the Empire, the Alhambra was reputed to have in residence two kinds of entertainers— the ballet girls arrayed in revealing costumes onstage and the more traditional varieties of "working girls" for hire (along with a fair number of their male equivalents, the "rent boys"), sauntering throughout the theatre. Both sorts of "professionals" were allegedly for sale, for the right price.

When the poet Arthur Symons, a Methodist minister's son, came to London and entered his first music hall, it was love—or at least infatuation—at first sight. In the early 1890s, he became friends with John Hollingshead, the Alhambra's manager. That entrée afforded him what he called later "the very key" that "could unlock . . . the gate of my Forbidden Paradise" (*Memoirs*, 110). He asked himself, "Did I . . . deliberately choose music-halls. . . or did they choose me? I imagine they chose me. I lived in them for the mere delight and the sheer animal excitement they gave me" (*Memoirs*, 109). The "delight" did not come from the shows alone at the Alhambra.

In his memoirs, which were published by Karl Beckson in 1989, forty-four years after his death, Symons reported that

> The first ballet girl I ever 'took up with' (as they always say) was Violet Pigott. . . . She was stupid, sensual, pretty and not perverse; she was slender and had shapely legs. When flesh means nothing more than the satisfaction of one's senses, she was nothing more to me than a thing of flesh. . . . Hating as I always did to wait for such creatures, and at so far a distance [she lived in the Chalk Farm Road], I remember strolling up and down a street near there, and to my intense delight buying the rare first edition of *Le Livre Mystique* of Balzac of 1835. . . .
>
> And as I write these lines I still feel that curious thrill I always had on finding before me a rare first edition; and how—at that time—such books meant—*de temps en temps*—ever so much more to me than these mere girls of the Alhambra. . . . I had nothing much to do in those years except to wander after sensations and adventures, after women and after books. (*Memoirs*, 113)

To wander after women who danced at the Alhambra Theatre and after books: that conjunction was no accident in Symons's case, for his pursuit of "animal excitement" through the music hall was also a literary pursuit. He turned his affairs with the ballet girls into poetry, along with his impressions of their performances. In his 1895 volume *London Nights,* issued by the avant-garde publisher and sometime purveyor of pornography, Leonard Smithers, Symons used verse to capture the sensations produced by lighting, costumes, and choreography, while at the same time boasting about his intimate knowledge of the women who were merely impersonal erotic spectacles to other men:

VII. ON THE STAGE

Lights, in a multi-colored mist,
From indigo to amethyst,
A whirling mist of multi-colored lights;
And after, wigs and tights,
Then faces, then a glimpse of profiles, then
Eyes, and a mist again;
And rouge, and always tights, and wigs, and tights.

You see the ballet so, and so,
From amethyst to indigo;
You see a dance of phantoms, but I see
A girl who smiles to me;
Her cheeks, across the rouge, and in her eyes
I know what memories,
What memories and messages for me.

(*London Nights,* 15)

Around the same time that he was enjoying his role as the Alhambra's designated stagedoor Johnny (or as Hollingshead called him affectionately, *"l'Enfant de la maison*" [*Memoirs*, 109]), Symons was involved in a relationship of quite a different sort, this one taking place largely on paper, in the form of letters to and from a young woman named Katherine Willard. Like Symons, Katherine Willard had a retired clergyman for a father, though hers was American. She was also the daughter of a lady who ran a finishing school in Berlin, as well as the niece of the American temperance reformer, Frances Willard. Irreproachably respectable and carefully brought up, she nevertheless harbored dreams of using her vocal training and natural gifts as the basis for a professional career in musical comedy. It was in regard to this ambition that Symons commented, with palpable dismay, in a letter of 21 December 1891:

> Few people are fonder of the stage than I am, or more interested in everything theatrical, but I don't quite like the idea of seeing you in it. It is not the fact of the acting, but the associations of every kind. . . . [For] the greater part of actresses on every stage are without even pretensions to virtue. . . . I used to think at one time that it was merely a Puritan prejudice to look on actors and actresses as specially immoral people. But now that I have so many opportunities of seeing for myself, I find that it is only the truth. They *are*, as a class, more uniformly immoral than any other class of people. (*Letters*, 91–92)

Symons's confidence that he could move among these supposed moral lepers unscathed, but that a lady could not, was hardly unique. At the end of the nineteenth century, London was filled with theatres. Gentlemen patronized them regularly and, moreover, had no qualms about frequenting every sort of entertainment, from melodramas to High Art plays to the tights-and-lights shows and semi-nude *tableaux vivants* at the music halls. Nor did middle or upper-class gentlemen hesitate to consort with dancers and other performers offstage.

Men of the lower-middle classes, whose hold upon respectability was more tenuous and thus needed to be protected more fiercely, looked with greater disfavor upon the stage and especially at anyone who went from being a spectator to a participant. In a wonderfully funny take-off of lower-middle-class suburban life, the 1892 comic novel *The Diary of a Nobody*, George and Weedon Grossmith (who were both actors themselves) satirized this Philistine attitude through their narrator. Mr. Pooter, a born office drone, wants his son to plod along in his footsteps and avoid the temptations of the footlights. But the younger Pooter, who has cast off the name of "Willie" and daringly renamed himself "Lupin,"

> informs me, to my disgust, that he has been persuaded to take part in the forthcoming performance of the 'Holloway Comedians.' He says he is to play Bob Britches in the farce, *Gone to my Uncle's*; Frank Mutlar is going to play old Musty. I told Lupin pretty plainly I was not in the least degree interested in the matter, and totally disapproved of amateur theatricals. (*Diary of a Nobody*, 96–97)

But even a clerk was allowed to sit through any show that he fancied (if and when he could afford to buy a ticket) without fear of being morally corrupted by it or of losing his pretentions to "gentlemanly" status.

The double standard of gender was never more rigid, however, than in the case of women's relationship to the theatre. Women of the lower-middle, the middle, and the upper classes—all those who were "ladies" or who might hope to lay claim to that title—not only were discouraged from going on the stage; they were also, in some instances, actively dissuaded by friends, family, clergy, and even by novelists and essayists from setting foot in the theatre at all. "But do you not see," John Ruskin had asked in his 1865 lecture "Of Queens' Gardens," that for a woman to fulfill her "true place and power" as the moral guardian of the home, she must be "enduringly, incorruptibly good?" Yet women, according to late-Victorian ideology, were easily corrupted and readily led astray—not merely by what they did, but by what they saw or heard. This was not the paranoid suspicion of a conservative minority; it was an article of faith for many a progressive, or even radical, thinker at the end of the nineteenth century.

George Moore, the Irish-born bohemian and author of fiction and essays, was powerfully drawn to the London stage and determined to raise it to a new level of excellence as a home for ideas, poetical language, and political debates. In the early 1890s, he joined forces with a transplanted Dutchman, J. T. Grein, to form the Independent Theatre Society, a subscription-only "private" club devoted to the production of work too avant-garde to appeal to the commercial instincts of the West End's actor-managers or to be licensed by the Censor in the Lord Chamberlain's Office. In his informal role as a scout for new plays, George Moore did not hesitate to contact the lesbian couple, Katherine Bradley and Edith Cooper, who wrote poetry together as "Michael Field" and to solicit from them a play, *A Question of Memory*, which was staged in 1893. But in his capacity as a novelist, he used the full force of psychological realism and narrative techniques learned from his reading of Émile Zola to argue for women's weakness of character and to demonstrate that they could not be trusted to go to the theatre even as spectators without jeopardizing their minds and their morals.

Moore's 1885 novel *A Mummer's Wife* told the story of a lower-middle-class woman's headlong decline into adultery, drunkenness, and eventually prostitution, all set into motion by her visit to a musical comedy theatre in a Northern pottery town. The experience unhinges her "febrile and vacillating imagination," and the narrator relates in clinical detail "with what abandonment of the senses, with what alienation of the brain, Kate threw herself into the enjoyment of the evening" (*Mummer's*, 137):

> The sparkling marriage chorus, with the fanciful peasants and the still more fanciful bridegroom in silk . . . dazzled and seduced Kate like a sensual dream, and in all she saw and felt there was a mingled sense of nearness and remoteness, a divine concentration, and an absence of her own proper individuality. Never had she heard such music

[15]

... The melting chords were as molten lead poured into her heart, and all her musical sensibilities rushed to her head like wine, it was only by a violent effort, full of acute pain, that she saved herself from raising her voice with those of the singers; and dreading a giddiness that might precipitate her into the pit, she remained staring blindly at the stage. (*Mummer's,* 133)

The female protagonist does manage to keep from flinging herself suicidally down from the gallery, but not (figuratively speaking) from beginning her descent into "the pit." In her case, the chief agent of destruction is the musical element of popular theatre, the sort of *"opera bouffe"* songs which Arthur Symons's friend and correspondent, Katherine Willard, longed to sing onstage. Such music

penetrated, winding and unwinding itself, into the deepest recesses of Kate's mind. It seduced like a deep slow perfume; it caressed with the long undulations of a beautiful snake and the mystery of a graceful cat. It went and it came, stretching forth invisible hands. . . . On the sweet current of the music she was carried far away, far beyond the great hills into a land of sleep, dream, and haze, and a wonderful tenderness swam within her as loose and as dim as the green sea depths that a wave never stirs. (*Mummer's,* 142)

How could any woman risk going to the theatre—and how could any father, brother, or husband dare to escort her—when she was likely not only to be "seduced," but to have her senses so stimulated that she would have an orgasm right there in her seat and forever be ruined by the experience?

Yet here lay the startling paradox of a late-Victorian lady's existence: it mattered relatively little whether or not she actually occupied a stall, for she could learn all about the theatre and become as familiar with its productions and its personalities as she liked, thanks to the publishing industry. Nothing barred her access to information about what was happening onstage or backstage, for such information was ubiquitous. It reached her through the fiction that she borrowed from the circulating libraries (or, after the early 1890s, when the one-volume novel superseded the triple-decker, that she purchased outright). It provided subject matter for the poetry she read in slim volumes or saw printed in periodicals. Magazines and newspapers, of course, were filled with items about plays, playwrights, actors, and actresses and often ran pages of related illustrations. Reviewers published their criticial opinions of each season's new offerings. The "Letters" columns fostered debates over issues such as the supposed immorality of the music halls or the censorship of Biblical plays by the Lord Chamberlain's Office. Occasionally, some periodicals even gave their readers special supplements, in the form of printed sheets that could be cut up and assembled into three-dimensional "toy theatres," reproducing the stage sets and costumes of hit plays. These miniature stages became the prized possessions of children—including little girls—who grew up thinking of the theatre as part of their everyday domestic life.

London's theatre world was as much a print phenomenon as it was a physical fact, and print circulated everywhere, to anyone who could afford it, as well as to everyone who encountered it accidentally. The very songs and airs which allegedly were so dangerous to a lady's virtue in a theatrical setting could be brought into her drawing-room as sheet music—sheet music which, moreover, was often graced with images of the same female performers (including those in the notorious music halls) from whom Arthur Symons so gallantly guarded Katherine Willard. Colorful posters and handbills with information about current productions and their stars greeted male and female passersby alike from walls both indoors and outdoors, wherever one went. Advertising of all kinds featured theatrical celebrities endorsing products from soap to cigarettes. Stage-related calendars, datebooks, paper fans, and other sorts of printed material turned up in Christmas stockings.

New sorts of publications appeared—series such as *Pearson's Photographic Portfolio of Footlight Favourites by Eminent Photographers,* which from December 1894 through March 1896 brought a sheaf of black-and-white portraits of male and female stars into purchasers' homes, in thirteen installments. The middle-class collecting mania of the 1890s fueled the financial success of such projects and led to ever more elaborate offerings of theatre-related material, including George Newnes's full-color gallery of pin-ups, *Celebrities of the Stage,* with breathless prose appreciations of current-day *artistes* supplied by Boyle Lawrence. Even the world of the music hall, though unsafe for a lady to enter, could be safely brought to her home through the publisher T. Fisher Unwin's "artistic" turn-of-the-century volume, *The "Halls."* George Gamble's introductory essay, "Chiefly Concerning the Music Halls," a surprisingly unfriendly account of the entertainments in question, began with this disclaimer:

> Mostly, a music-hall artiste is a person who is neither an artiste nor a performer in a hall of music: mostly, a music-hall artiste is a person who has less right of existence, either as fact or as name, than a pavement artiste; mostly, a music-hall artiste is a person who has to roar, bellow, screech, caterwaul for supremacy throughout a mere orchestral free-fight. (*The 'Halls,'* 9)

But if such expressions of indifference or hostility were meant to convince middle-class bookbuyers (particularly women) who had never seen a music-hall show that they had missed very little, that impression was countered by G. F. Scotson-Clark's bold and vibrant illustrations. These visual representations rendered Vesta Tilley, Marie Lloyd, George Robey, Dan Leno and other stars—even an animal act, called "Lockhart's Elephants"—as dynamic, appealing, and glamorous figures.

Print media gave "respectable" women access to every sort of theatrical spectacle and allowed them to feel connected to London's stageworld, whether they were among the lucky few who attended the theatre regularly or among the many who never went at all. Indeed, the more a new publishing venture wished to draw in female readers, the more likely it was to feature images and articles related to the stage, knowing that forbidden or even semi-forbidden fruits were well nigh irresistible.

The Bodley Head publishing firm's experimental art and literary quarterly, *The Yellow Book*, set out deliberately to engage the interest of sophisticated women readers. (How well it succeeded may be judged by the extraordinary number of female contributors it managed to attract, during its three-year run from 1894 to 1897.) With Henry Harland as literary editor and Aubrey Beardsley overseeing the art contents, the magazine launched itself in April 1894 with an issue brimming with stage-related works. The most significant of the theatrical components was supplied by "*The Fool's Hour*: The First Act of a Comedy." As its title suggested, this was the opening act of a play (one that was never completed or performed), written by George Moore and his *inamorata* of the moment, the "New Woman" novelist Pearl Mary Craigie (a.k.a. "John Oliver Hobbes"). The same issue contained a one-act play by Fred M. Simpson, titled *The Dedication*. But Max Beerbohm's satirical essay, "A Defence of Cosmetics," also discoursed at length upon the "grave insouciance" of the music-hall performer Cissie Loftus and weighed her charms against those of "clever malaperts" like Marie Lloyd and Ada Reeve ("Defence," 76–77). "Mercedes," the first of "Two Sketches" by *The Yellow Book's* literary editor, Henry Harland, included its narrator's memories of a visit to a theatre in Paris to see *Le Comte de Monte Cristo* and descriptions of his prized childhood possession, a "toy-theatre . . . [with] a real curtain of green baize, that would roll up and down, and beautiful colored scenery that you could shift, and footlights" ("Mercedes," 139.) A reproduction of Walter Sickert's painting, *The Old Oxford Music Hall,* gave the magazine buyer an excellent sense of how the stage and the orchestra looked from the gallery during a performance—a performance featuring a blonde-haired, short-skirt-wearing girl in the distant spotlight. Aubrey Beardsley's line drawing called *Portrait of Mrs. Patrick Campbell,* on the other hand, brought viewers close enough to the figure of the actress who recently had created a sensation in Pinero's *The Second Mrs. Tanqueray* to be able to inspect the ringlets of hair falling across her face. The contribution by short-story writer Hubert Crackanthorpe, although it actually had nothing to do with the stage, lured readers with the promise of its title, "Modern Melodrama," and with hints that the dying "fallen woman" at its center might have been an actress. Even *The Yellow Book's* back cover, designed by Beardsley, featured an image of heads, both masked and unmasked, which seemed to be posed in a theatre box and framed by its curtains (thus picking up wittily on the closing word of text of this first issue of the magazine, which was indeed "Curtain").

Meanwhile, thanks to a drop in the costs associated with printing and binding and the consequent increase in the 1890s of books in a one-volume, affordable format, publishers now could market new plays directly to the bookbuying public—a public which, of course, included women. Contemporary stageworks no longer lived for one short season, then vanished. Instead, they began to receive handsome presentations and to be treated as art.

In this, as in so many other literary phenomena, Oscar Wilde was in the vanguard, urging his publishers to give to the appearance of a single play the same attention they were accustomed to lavishing on a volume of poetry. Wilde realized, moreover, that readers would need some incentive to purchase what they already knew so much about, after encountering reviews by critics for the dailies and weeklies who tended (as film reviewers do now) to recount the plot and spoil all the best lines. Thus, he turned the stage directions for his plays into mini-lectures, mostly tongue-in-cheek, with elaborate disquisitions upon the characters that supplemented the action and, in a sense, compensated the reader for the loss of the pleasures associated with being in a theatre. (Today, we can find the equivalent of this marketing strategy in the so-called "directors' commentaries" used to entice customers to purchase DVD releases of popular films.)

These additions were created for and existed only on the page. Sometimes, they shamelessly flattered the reader, by requiring an unusual degree of historical or cultural knowledge. Such was the case with Wilde's epigrammatic asides about his characters for the 1899 publication of *An Ideal Husband,* where each figure was introduced in turn with reference to an artist of the past—Watteau, Vandyck, Boucher, Lawrence:

> MABEL CHILTERN is a perfect example of the English type of prettiness, the apple-blossom type. She has all the fragrance and freedom of a flower. . . . She has the fascinating tyranny of youth, and the astonishing courage of innocence. To sane people she is not reminiscent of any work of art. But she is really like a Tanagra statuette, and would be rather annoyed if she were told so. (*Ideal Husband,* 300)

In some instances, however, Wilde's additions to the published versions of his plays seemed to be directed explicitly toward a female reader, using information and allusions associated with feminine spheres of knowledge. Thus, Wilde wrote that "LADY MARKBY is a pleasant, kindly, popular woman, with grey hair à la marquise and good lace" (*Ideal Husband,* 301)—details unlikely to mean much to readers unfamiliar with the names of women's hairstyles or with differences in the grades of their accessories.

George Bernard Shaw, another Irishman who understood the value of tapping into lucrative new markets, went Wilde one better. Not only did he supply witty commentary upon his characters for the publication of his plays, but lengthy Prefaces, such as the one for his 1898 *Plays Pleasant and Unpleasant*—full-scale essays upon social or political matters, as well as rejoinders to critics who had failed to be converted by seeing his works onstage. Yet like Wilde, Shaw too seemed sometimes to be addressing women bookbuyers in particular. Thus, at the start of the published version of *Arms and the Man,* Shaw described his female protagonist's mother as "a woman over forty, imperiously energetic, with magnificent black hair and eyes, who might be a very splendid specimen of the wife of a mountain farmer, but is determined to be a Viennese lady, and to that end wears a fashionable tea gown on all occasions" (*Arms,* 126). Again, the social meaning of the character's choice of costume was likely to resonate more effectively with a female reader—and one, moreover, of a particular class.

Female bookbuyers of the Nineties, therefore, could find themselves in the odd position of feeling as though they knew all about the latest developments in the London theatre, while in many cases experiencing these only at secondhand, through print. Reading plays could make them as informed about the drama as were their brothers who attended the first nights—more informed, since they also had the benefit of the dramatists' post-production reflections. And consuming a text such as Leonard Merrick's 1898 novel, *The Actor-Manager*, could carry them beyond a mere stagegoer's perspective; it could give them an insider's view of how playwrights, actor-managers, and the members of a company worked together or failed to cooperate, as well as a scathing critique of the actor-manager system as a whole.

From Merrick's hero, a leading man and dramatist, and from his heroine, an educated but impoverished young woman who supports herself by acting, even those who rarely or never attended plays would have received up-to-date pronouncements on the need for theatrical reform of the kind that soon would inspire Harley Granville Barker and Lillah McCarthy, in their groundbreaking seasons at the Royal Court. As the character of Alma King says, "The great future for the Stage lies in perfect freedom: freedom to try every kind of experiment—to be realistic or idealistic, prosaic or fantastic, 'well made' or plotless; freedom to go anywhere . . . and do anything" (*Actor-Manager*, 17). Yet Merrick's narrative illustrates the painful irony of such lofty visions, particularly when spoken by a woman, who can dream of artistic liberty for the Stage, but who must remain the prisoner of gender restrictions from which men are immune. Almost as soon as Alma King articulates to her guest these bright hopes for the drama, her Cockney landlady bursts into the room. Finding a male visitor and assuming the worst, she turns Miss King out onto the street, shouting, "This is a respectable 'ouse—not meant for the likes of 'er!. . . . I might 'ave told what it'd be when I found you was an actress—I'd never 'ave taken you if I'd known!" (*Actor-Manager*, 19).

However well-informed late-Victorian female readers in general might have been by their immersion in theatre through the medium of print, there was nonetheless one category of woman who could not be satisfied with such secondhand knowledge alone: the would-be woman writer. If she were to enter the field of journalism or, especially, if she were to produce novels that reflected the current scene, she needed direct acquaintance with all varieties of modern life. The London theatre, of course, constituted one of the most important facets of contemporary experience. Thus, the heroine of the 1898 feminist novel, *A Writer of Books* by "George Paston" (pseudonym of Emily Morse Symonds), announces to the young man who is courting her, "'I'll tell you what I've been wanting to go to for months, and that is a music-hall. I may have to send my hero or my villain to one some day, and must get the local colour right.'" But her conventional and conservative middle-class suitor balks at the request to escort her there, unconsciously echoing the cautions of Arthur Symons to Katherine Willard about the musical comedy stage:

> 'I shouldn't like to take you to a place like that,' returned Tom reluctantly, yet with decision. 'I know ladies do go nowadays, and I daresay the programmes may be right enough. It's the company I'm thinking of. I shouldn't care to take any young lady I—I respected among such people. I wouldn't take my sister if I had one.' (*Writer of Books*, 103)

Only after their wedding does Tom finally grant her wish, for, as he explains, an unmarried girl cannot safely be brought into such an environment, but "'a married woman is different' (*Writer of Books*, 152).

Cosima, the novelist-in-training, approaches with "an almost childish feeling of anticipation" this opportunity to encounter an environment previously closed to her (*Writer of Books*, 152). Once in the theatre, however, she responds to the spectacle of lights, colors, and music very differently from Kate, the stage-infatuated protagonist created by a male author in George Moore's *A Mummer's Wife*. As Paston notes,

> The interior and decorations of the Golden Salon were more than equal to Cosima's expectations, but the performance was a cruel disappointment. The 'rattling good programme' struck her as the dreariest entertainment she had ever assisted at. As each turn came on, she expected the interest and amusement of the show to begin, but singers and dancers succeeded each other without adding any thing appreciable to the gaiety of the evening. The acrobats were clever, and some of the dancing was not ungraceful, but the only performers who rose to the heights of excellence were the dogs, who went through their various feats with a dignity, a conscientiousness, and an artistic enthusiasm which rendered the contrast between them and their human colleagues almost pathetic in its irony.
>
> In the intervals of the performance Cosima looked about her. She could not perceive that any members of the audience appeared to be enjoying themselves overmuch. (*Writer of Books*, 152–153)

On another occasion, Paston's heroine visits "a popular musical burlesque"—that is, a musical comedy of the sort in which Katherine Willard hoped to triumph and also of the kind which supposedly drove the female protagonist of *A Mummer's Wife* to a state of sexual frenzy. But it proves no more satisfactory than the entertainments geared toward the working classes:

> All seemed to her equally arid, inane, and vulgar.
>
> For two or three hours of this sort of thing, then, people were content to pay half-a-guinea, and actually imagined that they had gained a fair bargain. And these were London people, many of them rich, some of them noble; people who might insist on having the best that the world can give . . . and this was what they were willing to accept, this dreary farrago of barrel-organ tunes and Cockney fooling. (*Writer of Books*, 66)

[21]

At the same time, Cosima makes the acquaintance of an actress—one of those "creatures" whom Arthur Symons claimed to be able to pick up more easily than a rare book—and discovers to her astonishment that female stage performers are neither promiscuous nor uneducated. Indeed Bess Heywood, the actress in question, scorns the attentions of men, interests herself personally and politically only in the cause of womanhood, and reads Samuel Pepys, John Evelyn, and other early English diarists for enjoyment.

Emily Morse Symonds's novel is a rebuke to the views of George Moore in particular, and of contemporary male authors in general, on the subject of women's relationship to the theatre world. It is also a demystification of that world for the benefit of "respectable" female readers who were discouraged (if not barred) from experiencing the many varieties of theatre directly. Print media—whether periodicals, books, posters, or other ephemera—may have surrounded women with texts and images from the stage, just as the presence of such large numbers of licensed and unlicensed theatres throughout London shaped women's own sense of the physical and the ideological landscapes in which they moved. But in the end the stage, like many a masculine-controlled institution of the period, was not, according to Symonds's heroine, all that it was cracked up to be.

Did this mean that the message of turn-of-the-century feminism to women was to abandon their interest in theatre, whether on the stage or on the page, and to turn to other, more welcoming venues and genres? Quite the opposite. The first two decades of the twentieth century saw unceasing and successful activism designed to sweep away the taboos around "respectability" that often stood in the way of middle-class women's access to the theatre and to appropriate the stage for feminist political purposes. Emily Morse Symonds herself would go beyond her already transgressive role as a "New Woman" novelist to become a playwright, creating works such as *Clothes and the Woman* (1907) and *Tilda's New Hat* (1908) that took a caustic and comic look at female body image and gender attitudes. Elizabeth Robins and Cicely Hamilton not only would write pro-suffrage melodramas and comedies—such as, respectively, *Votes for Women!* and *How the Vote Was Won*—but organize the Actresses' Franchise League, to enlist the help and support of the working women of all classes who made their livings onstage.

These efforts, both on the page and on the stage, would give lie to the masculine fantasies of Symons's *London Nights,* which had dominated the literary world in the 1890s. Women of the theatre were more than "rouge, and always tights, and wigs, and tights." They were the political future, and they would not rest until they had won for themselves the same right that the heroine of Merrick's *The Actor-Manager* had demanded for the Stage: the "freedom to go anywhere . . . and do anything."

Gender and the London Theatre, 1880–1920

Savoy Theatre: To the Public.
Circular letter from Richard D'Oyly Carte, announcing the opening of the new theatre, 6 October 1881.

The modern age of London theatre began on an evening in 1881, with the flick of a switch. At eight o'clock p.m., the gas lights went off, and the new Savoy Theatre, constructed by Richard D'Oyly Carte in the Strand, suddenly was illuminated by twelve-hundred incandescent lamps. The Savoy, designed by the architect C. J. Phipps to hold 1,292 people, was the first public building in England lit entirely by electricity, and the production on that historic night of 6 October was Gilbert and Sullivan's *Patience,* which had been transferred from its successful run at the Opéra Comique and restaged with new scenery and costumes.

So momentous was the occasion—or rather, so momentous did D'Oyly Carte wish the public to believe this to be—that he wrote and had printed for distribution a four-page letter about it. In advertising to potential theatregoers the advantages of electric lamps, D'Oyly Carte emphasized the superiority of a light source which, unlike gas, gave off no "perceptible heat" or "foul" fumes. The effect, he promised, would be to create an atmosphere of "coolness" and, most important, of "purity." While never saying so directly, D'Oyly Carte clearly aimed his argument for this new kind of environment at ladies, as well as at the gentlemen who would escort them. Throughout the nineteenth century, the London theatre world in general had been associated with anything but "purity," whether of air or of morals. It had been a world that respectable women entered at their peril. But D'Oyly Carte's modern theatre, with its "private road" for the approach of theatregoers' carriages, its entrance with "a pavement under cover of seventy feet," its "refreshment saloons, retiring and cloak rooms," its trumpeting of adherence to fire regulations, and especially its "lounge for ladies on the stalls level," marketed itself as a safe and welcoming space for women of the upper-middle and aristocratic classes.

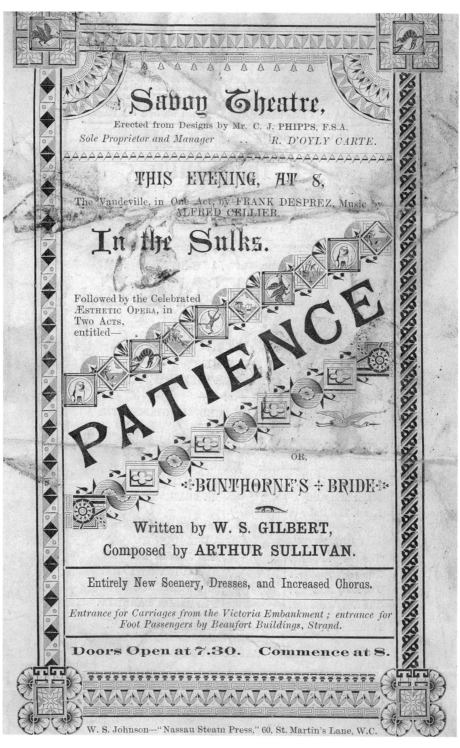

Program for *Patience* by W.S. Gilbert and Arthur Sullivan, [1881].

Program for *Patience, or Bunthorne's Bride*
by W.S. Gilbert and Arthur Sullivan,
produced at the Savoy Theatre, [1881].

Richard D'Oyly Carte promoted his Savoy Theatre as embodying a new kind of theatregoing experience in London, one which all other managers would want to copy. In his circular for the Savoy's opening, he predicted that soon all theatres, like his own, would be lit electrically and would feature other innovations, including a policy of paying ushers and cloakroom attendants a living wage, in order to eliminate the nuisance of employees "demanding or expecting" tips. But while D'Oyly Carte was forward-looking in his embrace of technology, his labor practices, and his breaking of gender taboos—explicitly inviting women to be patrons of his theatre and assuring them of a comfortable atmosphere—he held the line in terms of class. The modern theatre that he envisioned was designed chiefly with gentlemen and ladies in mind.

Fittingly, the first production brought to this new environment was Gilbert and Sullivan's *Patience,* which had premiered at the Opéra Comique in April 1881. Like the theatre building itself, *Patience* reflected a blend of innovative and retrogressive thinking. In subject matter, it was thoroughly up-to-date. W.S. Gilbert's libretto satirized the Pre-Raphaelites, the aesthetic movement, and the American painter J.M. Whistler, but especially the newest figure to emerge in London's art circles, the poet and critic Oscar Wilde. Recently down from Oxford, Wilde had made a splash with outrageous pronouncements and equally startling aesthetic garb. Gilbert's response was to lampoon Wilde as a mere *poseur,* affecting a "languid love of lilies." Walking his "flowery" way across the stage, the character of poet Reginald Bunthorne (played by George Grossmith, who later co-wrote the comic masterpiece, *The Diary of a Nobody*) became a well-known caricature of the new "effeminate" type of masculinity of the period. Less remembered, however, is that *Patience* was equally cutting toward educated young women with artistic interests, mocking them through the plaints of the "Twenty love-sick maidens we," whose "tastes have been etherealized" and rendered too "exalted" for romance with manly men.

Reginald Bunthorne, "Patience."
Cigarette card for Player's Cigarettes, issued by John Player & Sons, Nottingham, [early twentieth century].

Like the literary sphere of the same period, the theatrical world of 1880 to 1920 was intimately and indeed increasingly linked to the forces of marketing and consumerism. The same laughter at the expense of "unmanly" male aesthetes that sold tickets to performances of Gilbert and Sullivan's comic opera, *Patience,* could also be used to sell the Imperial Tobacco Company's wares. Produced to be collected and issued as part of a series of fifty, these turn-of-the-century cigarette cards devoted to characters from *Patience* echoed costume designs from the 1881 staging—designs which, in turn, had an earlier artistic referent. "Reginald Bunthorne," it was clear, was an amalgam of George du Maurier's caricatures of both J.M. Whistler and Oscar Wilde for *Punch,* that reliable mirror of mainstream Victorian resistance to the avant-garde. Bunthorne's head was based on Whistler's, while his costume and pose echoed Wilde's chosen styles of the 1870s and early 1880s—styles which challenged the conventions of masculinity.

On the reverse of this card (no. 23 of the series) appeared a lengthy account of the plot of *Patience.* Throughout the end of the nineteenth and the first part of the twentieth century (and even today), packs of cigarettes still were a cheaper indulgence for the middle and the working classes than were theatre stalls. (At the first night of *Patience* in the new Savoy Theatre, orchestra seats went for ten shillings and six pence, whereas "choice" brands of cigarettes, such as Cope's Bird's Eye, cost a mere three pence in the 1880s.) The popular dissemination, therefore, of detailed information about London theatre hits sometimes happened more through advertising gimmicks like these cards than through direct experience, especially for those who lived in the provinces. At the same time, the distribution of such cards helped to drum up business for theatres by bringing images from the stage into everyday life, creating a new sense that theatre had an accepted place in the routines of respectable households. This inter-dependence of art and commerce surely made it no coincidence that one feature of the new Savoy Theatre, as Richard D'Oyly Carte announced proudly in 1881, was a smoking-room.

MARK SAMUELS LASNER COLLECTION

Reginald Bunthorne, "Patience," cigarette card, [early twentieth century].

OSCAR WILDE.

Oscar Wilde, trade card, [ca. 1882–1883].

Oscar Wilde.
Trade card for "Economy" Folding Beds, New York, [ca. 1882–1883].

The costs associated with constructing or refurbishing buildings to bring in new technology, such as electrical lighting, meant that the late-Victorian London theatre could not afford to be self-contained. In order to expand profits and cover expenses, shows had to travel. During the earlier nineteenth century, they had done so throughout England. But as transatlantic crossings grew easier, tours in the U. S. offered increasingly lucrative returns. With a property such as Gilbert and Sullivan's *Patience*, though, Richard D'Oyly Carte faced a dilemma: how to recreate for American audiences the cultural context that explained the satire. It was easy for theatregoers in New York or Boston to understand why W. S. Gilbert would mock the "love-sick maidens" who made calves' eyes at poets. Laughter at the expense of blue-stockings and other female types associated with aspirations toward taste and learning had long been a staple of misogynist American humor. But how could he make them appreciate the jokes aimed specifically at Oscar Wilde and at Wilde's self-conscious violations of the norms of masculine dress and demeanor? After all, Wilde was still largely a local phenomenon, unfamiliar abroad.

D'Oyly Carte's solution was ingenious: he would pay Wilde to travel to the United States. Thus, in 1882 Wilde packed up his knee-breeches, velvet jackets, floppy ties, and patent-leather pumps and set off to declare nothing but his genius to the American Customs officers. Wherever he lectured on art and design, the reception he received was sensational; so, too, was the publicity that surrounded him. He soon eclipsed Reginald Bunthorne, his comical representation onstage, in fame and in public attention offstage. Indeed, his image—and the sophisticated, boundary-breaking version of masculinity emblematized by it—took on a life of its own. With no enforcement of trademark or copyright laws to stop them, commercial enterprises quickly appropriated Wilde as a marketing gimmick and sprinkled portraits of him throughout their advertisements, while refusing to compensate him. Oscar Wilde learned many lessons from this trip. Perhaps the most important was that public performance could provide the swiftest route to celebrity—a lesson that helped to push him eventually in the direction of writing plays that would use gender as a source of controversy.

Two photographs from *Princess Ida, or Castle Adamant*
by W. S. Gilbert and Arthur Sullivan,
produced at Bryn Mawr College, 1889.

Throughout his American lecture tour of 1882, Oscar Wilde negotiated a complex relationship with *Patience*. Although W. S. Gilbert's libretto reaffirmed conservative gender attitudes and equally conservative notions of art, Wilde used the personal notoriety which American productions of *Patience* lent him to attract audiences to his serious lectures on aesthetics and thus to create disciples. Early on, undergraduates at Bryn Mawr College forged a similarly uneasy bond with *Princess Ida*. Just as Wilde had recognized that he could more readily defang the satire in *Patience* by appropriating the role of the "effeminate" Bunthorne and critiquing it wittily than by distancing himself from it, so Bryn Mawr students found that they could best defuse this attack by the London theatre on "A woman's college! maddest folly going!" through a staging of Gilbert and Sullivan's 1884 opera on their own campus. Layers of comic irony abounded in this production, which was immortalized by the camera in 1889, with the casting of women undergraduates in all the roles. As well as achieving an almost Shakespearean dizziness of gender confusion—when, Hilarion, Cyril, and Florian disguise themselves as women, these three male characters are, after all, already being portrayed by women—this version of *Princess Ida* created a Sapphic subtext. W. S. Gilbert's concluding lyrics in praise of "The sway of Love" as more important than female higher education became not the intended celebration of heterosexual couples, but a paean to same-sex pairings, for only women filled the stage.

COLLEGE ARCHIVES, BRYN MAWR COLLEGE LIBRARY

Photographs from *Princess Ida* by W. S. Gilbert and Arthur Sullivan,
produced at Bryn Mawr College, 1889.

GIRL GRADUATES.

THEY intend to send a wire
        To the moon ;
And they'll set the Thames on fire
        Very soon ;
Then they learn to make silk purses
        With their rigs
From the ears of LADY CIRCE'S
        Piggy-wigs.
And weazels at their slumbers
        They'll trepan ;
To get sunbeams from cu*cum*bers
        They've a plan.
They've a firmly rooted notion
They can cross the Polar Ocean,
And they'll find Perpetual Motion
        If they can !

45

"Girl Graduates," in W. S. [William Schwenck] Gilbert, *Songs of a Savoyard*, [1890].

W. S. [William Schwenck] Gilbert
Songs of a Savoyard. Illustrated by the Author.
London: George Routledge and Sons, [1890].

W. S. Gilbert was, of course, the most celebrated writer of musical shows of the late-nineteenth century. (His earlier career as a dramatist never reached the same heights.) This volume, which capitalized on his fame by reprinting selected lyrics from his collaborations with the composer, Arthur Sullivan, also demonstrated Gilbert's surprising gifts as a visual artist. Had he not become England's best-known and best-paid satirist for the stage, he might well have held a position as a cartoonist for *Punch*. Indeed, he was wholly in sympathy with that magazine's tendency to bristle with disapproval at progressive developments, such as the emergence of middle-class women seeking higher education. Gilbert and Sullivan's *Princess Ida, or Castle Adamant* (1884) was in fact a reworking of Gilbert's earlier, non-musical play *The Princess*, which had been staged in 1870. Using Tennyson's poetic fantasy, *The Princess: A Medley* (1847), for its characters and plot, *Princess Ida* billed itself as "A Respectful Operatic Per-Version of Tennyson's 'Princess'" and burlesqued the Poet Laureate's work, while ridiculing women who abjured marriage in favor of learning and self-improvement. This copy of *Songs of a Savoyard* is open to Gilbert's image of one of the "girl graduates" whose "hearts are dead to men"—a high-minded figure in academic robes, foolishly resisting her male wooers.

Characters from *The Mikado, or the Town of Titipu*
by W. S. Gilbert and Arthur Sullivan.
Bronze, [early twentieth century].

The educated woman provided a continuing object of satire for W. S. Gilbert, who peppered various libretti with digs at the ridiculousness of Victorian girls' schooling. Although the targets of *The Mikado,* which premiered at the Savoy Theatre on 14 March 1885, ranged from the "music-hall singer" to the lady who "doesn't think she dances, but would rather like to try," Gilbert could not resist returning to a subject he had already explored in *Princess Ida* and asserting once again that a woman's true education began and ended with marriage. The immense popularity of the Gilbert and Sullivan operas led to the proliferation of turn-of-the-century souvenirs and collectibles. Among these was a bronze figurine of the pseudo-Japanese sisters, Yum-Yum, Pitti-Sing, and Peep-Bo, who declare themselves in song to be

> Three little maids who, all unwary,
> Come from a ladies' seminary,
> Freed from its genius tutelary.

Now at last "from scholastic trammels free," all await eagerly their opportunity to be brides.

   Although *Patience* (1881) had already mocked the aesthetic movement, which was noted for its interest in Japanese principles of art and design, Gilbert and Sullivan themselves helped to extend the orientalist craze with the success of *The Mikado.* Thus, ironically, they carried to mainstream audiences the tastes of such "effeminate" men as Oscar Wilde.

Shaksperean [sic] Show Book. With Original Literary Contributions, Illustrations, and Music . . . all Specially Contributed "For Charity."
[London, 1884].

Long before conquering the West End with a string of plays in the 1890s, Oscar Wilde (1854–1900) immersed himself in the theatre, chiefly by studying actresses' performances and cultivating their friendship. Ellen Terry, England's greatest female tragedian, inspired him to write poems such as "Under the Balcony." Its ambiguous opening line, "O Beautiful star with the crimson mouth!" ostensibly addressed to a heavenly body, seemed equally to describe the "star" of London's Shakespearean stage. (An anonymous parody in the *Pall Mall Gazette* of 3 June 1884 made the association explicit, rendering the line as "Beautiful star with the crimson lips/ And flagrant daffodil hair.")

Wilde's poem appeared in this souvenir book, issued as the program for the "Shaksperean [sic] Show" staged at the Royal Albert Hall from 29–31 May 1884. The charity event, which boasted a list of royal patrons and drew the participation of writers such as Tennyson and Browning, as well as artists from George Cruikshank to Walter Crane, was produced as a benefit to pay off the £5,000 mortgage of the Chelsea Hospital for Women. A note in this volume reported that "On the 24th day of May, in all the chief London, and some of the provincial Theatres, a special announcement of the Show was placed in every Box, Stall, and Dress Circle seat, by the kind courtesy of the proprietors or managers," thereby strengthening a growing link between the theatre and the worlds of aristocracy and of "High Art."

MARK SAMUELS LASNER COLLECTION

Program for *An Ideal Husband* by Oscar Wilde,
produced at the Theatre Royal Haymarket, [1895].

It took an Irish gentleman to expose the unsatisfactoriness of English gentlemen—
not only as husbands, but as politicians—and to do so in a way that made the criticism palatable to London theatregoers. Like *Lady Windermere's Fan* (1892) and *A
Woman of No Importance* (1893) before it, Wilde's 1895 comic melodrama blasted
gender "ideals" of many kinds, including such stifling notions as the need to sepa-
rate good women from bad ones, and championed Style (with a capital "S") as the
only necessary virtue. The program for *An Ideal Husband* scarcely exaggerated in la-
beling this "A New and Original Play of Modern Life."

   An Ideal Husband opened on 3 January 1895 at the Theatre Royal Haymarket,
which was managed by Herbert Beerbohm Tree. While Tree was in America, where
he made the shrewdest business decision of his life by acquiring the rights to *Trilby*,
the Haymarket was being run by the actor-managers H.H. Morrell and Lewis
Waller. The latter not only produced Wilde's new play, but starred in it as Sir Robert Chiltern, the less-than-ideal husband of the title. In the role of Lady Chiltern, he
cast Julia Neilson, who had already scored a success in *A Woman of No Importance*.
Four years earlier, Neilson had married Fred Terry, younger brother of Ellen Terry
(and also of the actresses Kate, Marion, and Florence Terry), thus consolidating the
dominance of the extended Terry clan on the London stage.

MARK SAMUELS LASNER COLLECTION

[Oscar Wilde]
The Importance of Being Earnest: A Trivial Comedy for Serious People. By the Author of
Lady Windermere's Fan.
London: Leonard Smithers, 1899.

Wilde's comedy turned British society upside down—or rather, inside out—with its strategy of constant inversion of everything from stage conventions to gender roles to the order of words in common platitudes. Its success was immediate, when it opened on 14 February 1895 at the St. James's Theatre, barely one month after *An Ideal Husband.* But Wilde's enemies (as well as members of his homosexual male coterie) thought they saw hints in it of "inversion" of a different kind. These suspicions shortly were confirmed. In the spring of 1895, Wilde brought a libel action against the Marquess of Queensberry for describing him as a "sodomite," lost that suit, and was in turn prosecuted by the Crown for the crime of committing "gross indecency" with men. The case against Wilde was more than a personal tragedy; it also meant disaster for the London theatre world in general. All of Wilde's works playing in the West End closed, an immense financial loss to actor-managers such as George Alexander (1858–1918), who was starring in and producing *Earnest.*

Following his conviction and imprisonment, Wilde wrote no further plays. But after he emerged from two years at hard labor, his writings gradually returned to public view, if not immediately to the stage. In 1899, the publisher (and sometime pornographer) Leonard Smithers issued *Earnest* in book form, omitting Wilde's name from the title-page and identifying the writer only as the author of the 1892 hit, *Lady Windermere's Fan.*

MARK SAMUELS LASNER COLLECTION

The Importance of Being Earnest. Mr. George Alexander, Miss Stella Patrick Campbell, and Miss Rosalie Toller, Mr. Allan Aynesworth.
Postcard photograph by the Daily Mirror Studio, advertising the production at the St. James's Theatre, [1909].

Oscar Wilde's arrest and imprisonment in April 1895 shook the London theatre. Many a playwright noted that Wilde's literary works, as much as his sexual conduct, had been on trial and feared that a new spirit of censorship and repression was in the air. Many an actor or male patron of the theatre felt, too, that it was safer for a time to keep a low profile or repair to France, in case widespread roundups for "gross indecency" ensued. But the most immediate effect of Wilde's catastrophe was to deprive the stage of his successful and profitable plays. For the last month of its run, *Earnest*—which had only just premiered in February 1895—continued with its author's name removed from all programs and signs; then, in early May, it closed.

After Wilde's death in 1900, his reputation slowly recovered and new productions of his plays appeared. The *Earnest* of 1909, however, was a revival featuring George Alexander, producer and star of the original. Fresh actresses—Rosalie Toller and Stella Campbell, the daughter of Mrs. Patrick Campbell—succeeded Irene Vanbrugh and Evelyn Millard, while the first Jack Worthing and Algernon Moncrieff returned in their roles. But as this postcard advertising the revival cruelly shows, Wilde's young gentlemen now needed something more than the help of pink shades to pass as young. George Alexander had reached his fifty-first year, and Allan Aynesworth (1865–1959) was fully forty-four (though not, to paraphrase Gwendolen Fairfax, more than usually plain).

MARK SAMUELS LASNER COLLECTION

The Importance of Being Earnest. Mr. George Alexander, Miss Stella Patrick Campbell, and Miss Rosalie Toller, Mr. Allan Aynesworth, postcard photograph, [1909].

Aubrey Beardsley, *The Woman in the Moon*, in Oscar Wilde, *Salome*, 1907.

Oscar Wilde
Salome: A Tragedy in One Act. Translated from the French of Oscar Wilde. With Sixteen Drawings by Aubrey Beardsley.
London: John Lane, 1907.

Wilde, who died in 1900, never lived to see *Salome* on the London stage. The pseudo-Biblical setting of his 1892 play gave the Lord Chamberlain's Office all the excuse it needed to shut down the early rehearsals at the Palace Theatre, where *Salome* was to have been produced in French with the nearly fifty-year-old Sarah Bernhardt as the virginal young princess. It still made its mark in sophisticated London circles, however, through the 1894 translation (attributed, in the book's dedication, to Wilde's lover, Lord Alfred Douglas) issued by Elkin Mathews and John Lane at the Bodley Head—an instance of successful "closet drama" in more ways than one. To encounter the play in this format was still quite an experience, thanks to the visual contributions of Aubrey Beardsley (1872–1898), in one of his first high-profile assignments as a book designer and illustrator. His pen-and-ink drawings of the characters went even further than the text in blurring gender distinctions and rendering the figures sexually ambiguous, if not hermaphroditic. They also offered their own wry commentary upon the dramatist, through uncomplimentary caricatures of Wilde's wide, moonlike visage and androgynous appearance.

The 1907 edition shown here, which followed the deaths of both Wilde and Beardsley, included all the illustrations and also supplied information about the first London production of the play in 1905, by the New Stage Club at the Bijou Theatre, Bayswater. It also substituted for the rather restrained front cover of the original a Beardsley design that used a peacock-feather motif, in order to signal exoticism and decadence within.

BRYN MAWR COLLEGE LIBRARY

[41]

Miss Maud Allan as "Salome," postcard photograph, [1908].

Miss Maud Allan as "Salome."
Postcard photograph by Rotary Photographic Co., London, [1908].

The urge to vilify and persecute anyone who used the stage to challenge sexual mores did not die out with the passing of the Victorian Age in 1901. Wilde's career as a dramatist was destroyed in 1895 by the prosecution for "gross indecency," after his failed lawsuit against the Marquess of Queensberry. So, too, the career of "Maud Allan" (1873–1956), a dancer from Canada originally named Beulah Durrant, was wrecked by the lawsuit she felt compelled to bring against Noel Pemberton Billing in 1918, after he accused her of lesbianism and other practices associated with the "Cult of Wilde." Billing, a reactionary political figure in Parliament, saw that he had an easy target, since Allan's fame in London long had rested on her public connections with Wilde's *Salome.* Not only did she score a huge success at London's Palace Theatre in 1908 with her expressive dance solo called *The Vision of Salome* (based on her interpretation of the protagonist of Wilde's play), but in April 1918 she also starred in Wilde's drama for a special one-performance revival by J.T. Grein at the Royal Court. Shockingly, even after World War I, Wilde's articulation of female desire still had the power to shock. The verdict against Allan and in favor of Billing turned not on the merits of the case (which were non-existent), but on the court's revulsion toward Wilde's play and toward any woman who would enact such an "immoral" role as that of Salome. Yet, by 1918, the same vampish persona that Allan had created in 1908, inspired by Wilde's murderous virgin, could be seen on every cinema screen in England, thanks to the American films of Theda Bara.

[43]

Henrik Ibsen
A Doll's House: Play in Three Acts. Translated by William Archer.
London: T. Fisher Unwin, 1889.

Two events in late-Victorian stage history marked the arrival of the modern age (and both were recognized immediately as turning-points). One was the flicking on of a switch at Richard D'Oyly Carte's Savoy Theatre in 1881 to illuminate an English public building for the first time with electric light; the other was the slamming of a door offstage to signal Nora Helmer's abandonment of husband, children, and home at the conclusion of the 1889 London production of *A Doll's House*. It would be difficult to say which moment caused a greater collective gasp among the assembled spectators or which ultimately proved more influential.

By happy accident, William Archer (1856–1924) learned Norwegian while visiting relatives in Norway and, by even happier accident, on one of his stays there discovered the works of Ibsen. Back in London, Archer played a central role in the growing circle of Ibsenites, an almost cult-like group that overlapped with socialists of the 1880s, as well as with those examining the "Woman Question." Two earlier versions of *A Doll's House* (one with Herbert Beerbohm Tree) were staged in London before 1889. But it was the production at the Novelty Theatre with Janet Achurch (1864–1916) as Nora which took the public, the critics, and a new generation of English playwrights by storm and which was commemorated in this photographically illustrated volume. Shown here is one of 115 large paper copies of William Archer's translation, which featured a frontispiece portrait of Henrik Ibsen and several views of Achurch in costume.

MARK SAMUELS LASNER COLLECTION

Janet Achurch as Nora, in Henrik Ibsen, *A Doll's House*, 1889.

"Oh, you prillil squillikins!"

Bernard Partridge, *"Oh, you prillil squillikins!,"* in F. Anstey, *Mr. Punch's Pocket Ibsen*, 1893.

F. Anstey [Thomas Anstey Guthrie]
Mr. Punch's Pocket Ibsen: A Collection of Some of the Master's Best-Known Dramas, Condensed, Revised, and Slightly Re-Arranged for the Benefit of the Student. With Illustrations by Bernard Partridge.
London: William Heinemann, 1893.

Satire, parody, and caricature have always been excellent gauges of the cultural importance of the things they mock, but never more so than at the end of the nineteenth century, when the popular press and the bookstalls alike were filled with comical versions of Henrik Ibsen's plays. Of Ibsen's dramas, the one ridiculed most energetically in England was *A Doll's House.* Along with *Ghosts* (which dared to bring onstage the subject of sexually transmitted disease), this play touched the rawest nerve, with its depiction of a wife and mother relinquishing her domestic role and leaving home to educate herself about life. "F. Anstey"—actually, Thomas Anstey Guthrie (1856–1934), a novelist who contributed many comic efforts to *Punch*—created a heroine for his "Nora; Or, the Bird-Cage," who does not quite manage to make it out the doll's house door at the end. Instead, having determined that she will begin her self-education "with a course of the Norwegian theatres," for "If *that* doesn't take the frivolity out of me, I don't really know what *will!*" Anstey's Nora decides to stay on awhile, since "the Norwegian theatres are all closed at this hour—and so I thought I wouldn't leave the cage till to-morrow—after breakfast." Reproduced here is Bernard Partridge's drawing of a very strong-minded Nora in her gypsy costume telling off her husband Torvald, who has had a few drinks too many at their party.

MARK SAMUELS LASNER COLLECTION

Max Beerbohm
Mr. William Archer.
Pencil, ink, and watercolor, [1896].

The late-Victorian theatre saw the rise of two cults simultaneously: the worship of Ibsen and the worship of Shakespeare. Both had their scholarly, as well as their performance-oriented sides; both often featured women in prominent roles (in some cases, quite literally). But both, too, were dominated by men. The support of "New Women" and of feminist causes professed, for instance, by British Ibsenites in the abstract never seemed to alter the conventional gender hierarchies in practice.

If William Archer (1856–1924) hadn't stumbled upon Ibsen's works, while he was visiting relatives in Norway, he would have had to invent them. In a sense, he did so anyway. As their chief translator into English and also as the advocate for them through his pronouncements in his drama criticism for *The World*, Archer was at the center of defining how Ibsen's plays would be received on the London stage. Although an admirer of the new movement in drama that the production of Ibsen's plays inspired, the more cool-headed Max Beerbohm was unsympathetic to slavish adoration of any sort. He could only look on with wonder and laugh at Archer's passion, depicting him in this caricature for the October 1896 *Chap-Book* as the humble supplicant before Ibsen's grim and rather ugly bust.

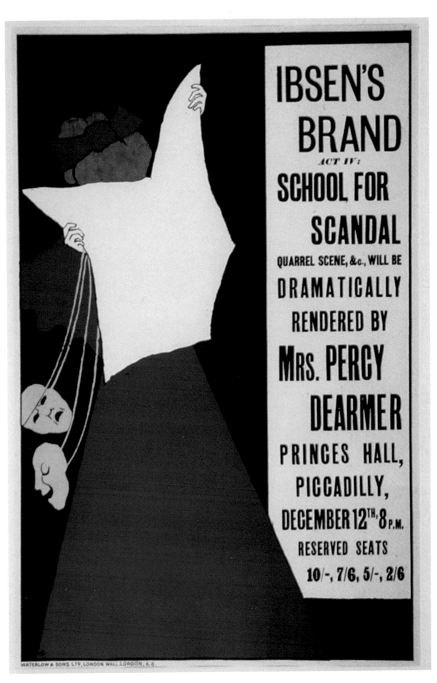

1. Mabel Dearmer, Poster for Ibsen's *Brand,* Act IV; *School for Scandal,* Quarrel Scene, &c, Dramatically Rendered by Mrs. Percy Dearmer, Princes Hall, Piccadilly, color lithograph, [ca. 1895].

11. Albert Morrow, Poster for *The New Woman* by Sydney Grundy,
color lithograph, [1897].

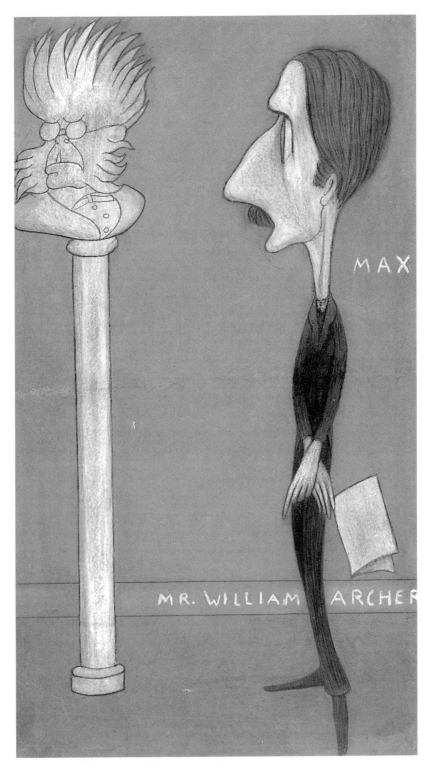

Max Beerbohm, *Mr. William Archer*, pencil, ink, and watercolor, [1896].

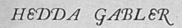

HEDDA GABLER

HENRIK IBSEN

Henrik Ibsen, *Hedda Gabler*, 1891.

Henrik Ibsen
Hedda Gabler: A Drama in Four Acts. Translated from the Norwegian by Edmund Gosse.
London: William Heinemann, 1891.

In his essay "Is the Theatre a Place of Amusement?" for the February 1900 issue of *Beltaine*, the "Organ of the Irish Literary Theatre" edited by W. B. Yeats, George Moore reported with disgust that the 1891 London production of *Hedda Gabler* "did not pay its expenses, although every one who went to see it was interested and pleased; every one left the theatre talking eagerly of the characters, the incidents, and the motive of the play." To Moore, an Irish novelist whose own venture into playwriting, *The Strike at Arlingford,* went almost unnoticed, the failure of Ibsen's *Hedda* to make money—at the very moment when Henry Arthur Jones's melodrama *The Dancing Girl* was reaping huge profits—merely confirmed his poor opinion of audiences in England. The theatregoers there, he wrote, sought and deserved nothing better than "the distraction of scenery, dresses, limelight, artificial birds singing in painted bowers."

But if the version of *Hedda* that opened in April 1891 at the Vaudeville Theatre could not be called profitable, it certainly proved memorable for the amount of negative attention it generated. Critics ransacked their store of adjectives in search of new ways to describe how foul, repellent, and unwomanly they found Ibsen's suicidal protagonist, played by the American-born actress, Elizabeth Robins (1862–1952). Meanwhile, the London-based coterie of English Ibsenites split over the translation undertaken by the poet and critic Edmund Gosse (1849–1928), with William Archer, his fellow Ibsen-worshiper and rival translator, leading the attack. William Heinemann's edition of the Gosse translation featured a portrait of Elizabeth Robins in the role of Hedda on the cover—perhaps not a surprising choice, considering that Heinemann (like Archer) was known to be romantically interested in the actress. This copy belonged to Robins herself.

MARK SAMUELS LASNER COLLECTION

Ibsen-Echegaray Performances.
Prospectus for Elizabeth Robins's productions of *Little Eyolf* by Henrik Ibsen and
Mariana by José Echegaray.
[London, 1896].

Male playwrights working in experimental modes disliked the late-Victorian actor-
manager system, for it concentrated all decisions about acceptance and rejection in
one person. Actor-managers were often conservative and cautious in their tastes. As
performers, they wanted flattering roles that appealed to, not risked alienating,
their fan-base; as the ones leasing theatres and running companies, they always put
the need to make money above any interest in breaking theatrical ground. But the
real disadvantage of the dominance of actor-managers was felt by women, whether
as actresses, playwrights, or designers. Already assumed by English society to be
"fallen," because of their affiliation with the theatre, women were doubly vulnera-
ble to harassment by heterosexual actor-managers, whose power was absolute.

Among those who spoke out openly against the control of theatres by actor-
managers was the feminist actress and writer originally from Kentucky, Elizabeth
Robins. While not the only woman to succeed in moving between the roles of performer and director/producer, she was certainly one of a small number. In the mid-
Nineties, she joined with another actress, Marion Lea, to bring European plays to
London audiences. Their production of Ibsen's *Little Eyolf* played for five performances at the Avenue Theatre in November 1896, with different actresses—including Florence Farr, Janet Achurch, and Mrs. Patrick Campbell—in the cast. It was
followed by five performances of Echegaray's *Mariana* at the Court Theatre in February 1897. Underwriting these productions was a subscription arrangement, coor-
dinated by Gerald Duckworth (the half-brother of Virginia Woolf).

MARK SAMUELS LASNER COLLECTION

Mabel Dearmer
Poster for Ibsen's *Brand,* Act IV; *School for Scandal,* Quarrel Scene, &c, Dramatically
Rendered by Mrs. Percy Dearmer, Princes Hall, Piccadilly.
Color lithograph, [ca. 1895]. [PLATE I]

One of the most delightful and unjustly forgotten turn-of-the-century British figures, Mabel Dearmer (a.k.a. Mrs. Percy Dearmer) had enough energy and talent
for any three people, let alone for an ambitious late-Victorian woman who was also
discharging the conventional duties of a wife and mother. An active participant in
socialist and suffragist societies and a member of the avant-garde *Yellow Book* magazine circle, Dearmer (1872–1915) seldom met a progressive social cause she didn't
like or, for that matter, an art form at which she couldn't excel. After receiving only
a short period of training by the painter Sir Hubert Von Herkomer (1849–1914),
she married and, when obliged to become a working wife in order to help support
her family, built a career as a professional book illustrator and poster artist. She also
discovered her ability to write and turned out poetry, novels, children's stories, and
eventually plays. Especially after 1910, she devoted herself to composing and staging a series of Christian Mystery plays, for theatre was her passion. Originally, she
had entertained dreams of stardom on the stage, but her poster for this evening of
theatrical excerpts stands as a record of one of her few public attempts at acting.
Had she lived longer, she might have fulfilled the prophecy of a stagehand who
worked with her on producing her Mystery plays and who—according to a posthu-
mous memoir of her by Stephen Gwynn—"gave her fifteen years to have a theatre
of her own." But she died prematurely of typhoid during World War I, after volun-
teering to join a women's medical corps and being shipped off to Serbia.

MARK SAMUELS LASNER COLLECTION

George Moore
The Strike at Arlingford: Play in Three Acts.
London: Walter Scott, 1893.

George Moore (1852–1933), an Irishman who owed his education in style to Paris, had already tried—and failed—to reform the English novel. In 1885, he used the pamphlet *Literature at Nurse, or Circulating Morals* to rail against the stranglehold of Mudie's and other circulating libraries on the distribution of fiction, a monopoly which enabled them to impose on authors their own standards for "acceptable" situations and language. Moore's polemic was published by Vizetelly & Co. (the firm that first gave Zola's works to England in translation), which in 1885 also issued his novel, *A Mummer's Wife: A Realistic Novel,* described by the reviewer for *The Pall Mall Gazette* as a "study of the decline of a woman, who quits middle-class respectability to plunge into theatrical bohemianism."

Moore steeped himself in "theatrical bohemianism" even before he began writing plays. In the more fluid sphere of the stage, too, he saw greater possibilities for change than in the established world of the novel. With J.T. Grein (and with William Archer, the drama critic and translator of Ibsen, as adviser), he organized the Independent Theatre Society, which dedicated itself to finding and producing plays of high literary quality that would attract sophisticated subscribers. Its other purpose was to challenge the mediocrity of the popular stage, where the censorship of the Lord Chamberlain's Office and the anti-Ibsen biases of the drama critic for *The Daily Telegraph,* Clement Scott (1841–1904), held sway. Moore's own effort for the Independent Theatre was *The Strike at Arlingford,* which was produced in February 1893 at the Opéra Comique. A heavy-handed treatment of social issues, involving the doomed love between a male socialist-activist and a female capitalist set against the backdrop of a labor uprising, the play succeeded in bringing new political types (including a middle-class woman who fights for workers' rights) to the stage, but failed to interest audiences. Moore inscribed this copy of the first edition to Olga Nethersole (1870–1951), who became one of a small number of important female actor-managers, taking control first of the Royal Court Theatre and later of Her Majesty's, the Adelphi, and the Shaftesbury.

MARK SAMUELS LASNER COLLECTION

Program for *A Question of Memory*
by Michael Field [Katherine Harris Bradley and Edith Emma Cooper], produced
by the Independent Theatre Society at the Opéra Comique, 27 October [1893].

George Moore often served as a "scout" for the Independent Theatre in its early
years, writing letters to authors and invading their drawing-rooms in search of suit-
ably avant-garde and serious plays. For Moore, this was a hunt with more than one
agenda, for he was especially keen on contacting and recruiting good-looking
women playwrights. Indeed, he used the subject of theatre and the possibility of
theatrical production as a means of flirtation and seduction. With Pearl Mary
Craigie (1867–1906), the "New Woman" novelist who published as "John Oliver
Hobbes," he went so far as to collaborate on the fashionable comedy *The Fool's
Hour*, the first act of which appeared in the April 1894 *Yellow Book*, but which was
left unfinished after it became clear that Craigie wanted no affair with him.

Play-hunting also brought Moore to the door of Katherine Bradley (1846–1914)
and Edith Cooper (1862–1913), authors of a published but unproduced play,
William Rufus, which he had read and admired. After his first meeting with the two
women who wrote together as "Michael Field," Moore sent a note addressed to
both, saying, "I daresay you saw that I was much interested in you—my face is
most indiscreet, it tells all my feelings far better than my pen." But if he got no-
where romantically with this aunt-and-niece lesbian couple, whose hearts belonged
to one another, he did succeed in acquiring a literary property from them for the
Independent Theatre Society. Their play *A Question of Memory* was staged by J.T.
Grein in October 1893.

MARK SAMUELS LASNER COLLECTION

Michael Field [Katherine Harris Bradley and Edith Emma Cooper].
Photograph by Bromhead, Clifton, Bristol, [ca. 1883–1889].

The two women who called themselves "Michael Field" were almost as much in love with the theatre as they were with one another. Their first affection was for Shakespeare. Dedicated scholars, they immersed themselves in English history and wrote their own Shakespearean blank verse in closet dramas such as *Fair Rosamund* (1897), their version of the marital conflict between Henry II and Eleanor of Aquitaine. Like a number of their works, this play was published in a format designed by Charles Ricketts (1866–1931), who in the second half of his life went on to be an important stage designer, creating costumes worn by Lillah McCarthy and sets for Harley Granville-Barker's productions, as well as both sets and costumes for G. B. Shaw's *St. Joan* (1924).

The only play, however, by "Michael Field" to be realized onstage was not a Shakespearean pastiche, but an attempt at drama about mid-nineteenth-century political crises abroad. *A Question of Memory* posed wrenching questions about individual responsibility in times of civil war, when patriotism clashes with the duty to keep loved ones safe. Set in a Hungarian village during the rebellion against the Austrian Empire, the action involved the sacrifices of women—some willing, others not—for the sake of a cause.

For "Michael Field," the experience of seeing their work produced by J. T. Grein's Independent Theatre was not a happy one. They found the play's pairing with François Coppée's *Le Pater* more than unsuitable; it was, they wrote in their journal, "exquisitely laughable . . . and we sent to Grein a letter that expressed our wrath at his blunder—blunder inartistic as it is ludicrous." Nothing seemed to go well after that. On the day after the disastrous first night of 27 October 1893, they recorded grimly, "It seems more natural to be dead than alive. We wake to the surprise of finding every morning paper against us." It could only cause acute pain to remember their friend Oscar Wilde's fanciful, if well-meant sentiments, on first hearing that the work was to be staged: "I look forward to listening to your lovely play recited on a rush-strewn platform, before a tapestry, by gracious things in antique robes, and, if you can manage it, in gilded masks."

MARK SAMUELS LASNER COLLECTION

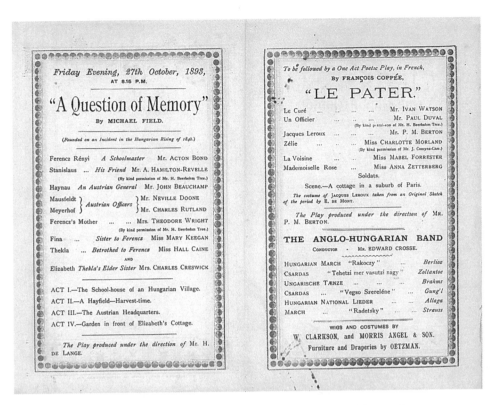

Program for *A Question of Memory* by Michael Field, [1893].

Michael Field [Katherine Harris Bradley and Edith Emma Cooper],
photograph, [ca. 1883–1889].

· ARTHVR · SYMONS ·

Robert Bryden, *Arthur Symons,* in William Archer, *Poets of the Younger Generation,* 1902.

William Archer
Poets of the Younger Generation. With Thirty-three Full-Page Portraits from Wood-
cuts by Robert Bryden.
London: John Lane, 1902.

Even if one never set foot on stage, designed a set or costume, or wrote a line of dialogue, it was possible to be an intimate of London theatre circles at the turn of the
century, especially if one were male. The roles of literary agent, adviser to theatre
managers, and a host of other less-defined positions were open to men who wished
to hang about backstage and socialize with performers. But the surest way to gain
access was to be a critic. In 1892, the poet and essayist Arthur Symons (1865–1945)
gave himself the pseudonym "Silhouette" and became a reviewer for the *Star*, writing about the London music halls for that newspaper. The appointment offered
him the perfect opportunity to meet and sleep with chorus girls every night, even as
he devoted his days to the pursuit of poetry through membership in the Rhymers'
Club. At the same time, he tried his hand as a playwright with a one-acter, *The Minister's Call,* based on a short story by Frank Harris. Like *A Question of Memory* by
"Michael Field," Symons's play was staged by J. T. Grein's Independent Theatre Society. Its opening in March 1892 was star-studded, with George Moore, John Lane
(Symons's publisher), Henry James, and Oscar Wilde attending. But it was not a
hit, and no further plays by Symons were produced in the Nineties.

Afterwards, Symons concentrated instead upon recording his impressions of the
theatrical milieu he loved—especially its feminine component—doing so in reviews, essays, poems, and short stories. The most famous of these stories was
"Esther Kahn," published in *The Smart Set* (October 1902). Although a work of fiction, it reflected in indelicate detail his own affair with a Jewish actress, whom he
saw first in the world of the Yiddish theatre which flourished in London's East End
immigrant community. Symons's short story was progressive in its willingness to
take seriously a woman's professional ambitions and desire to turn herself into a
great actress (and doubly progressive, because it employed a Jewish heroine). Yet it
was also backward-looking in its reaffirmation of the old cliché that the true source
of education for a woman artist could only be heterosexual experience and disap-
pointment in love.

[59]

Max Beerbohm
Mr. Henry Arthur Jones, England's Scourge.
Pencil, ink, and watercolor, [1907].

J. T. Grein, George Moore, "Michael Field," and other supporters of the Independent Theatre Society were not the only figures in the final decade of the nineteenth
century to push the London stage toward a more robust engagement with new and
challenging social ideas. As Henry Arthur Jones (1851–1929) said in the Preface to
his 1895 volume of essays, *The Renascence of the English Drama*, "I have fought for
the recognition of the distinction between the art of the drama on the one hand and
popular amusement on the other, and of the greater pleasure to be derived from the
art of the drama." Throughout the 1880s and 1890s, Jones walked a fine line between writing for intellectually sophisticated audiences and creating theatre with
mass appeal that drew in the crowds sought by the commercially minded actor-
managers of the West End. Like Pinero's melodramas (to which his stage works often were compared), Jones's plays were a boon to actresses. His 1891 *The Dancing-
Girl* gave Julia Neilson her star-making role and, by coincidence, a husband. (She
married Fred Terry—the brother of Ellen—who was also in the cast.) Yet Jones was
no feminist, as he proved with his not-wholly-funny comedy *The Case of Rebellious
Susan*, which debuted at the Criterion Theatre in October 1894 and recommended
that women settle marital discord by capitulating to their husbands and forgiving
their indiscretions.

   In this 1907 caricature, Max Beerbohm shows the playwright rather tentatively
waving a miniature American flag—an allusion to the laurels he had recently collected from Harvard University, which had bestowed on him an honorary degree.
But Beerbohm's title for this drawing, "Henry Arthur Jones, England's Scourge," is
wholly ironic. Jones's perspectives were often conservative and aligned with his
bourgeois British audiences' values. Although G. B. Shaw, the Irish radical, really
did apply a "scourge" to his adopted country, Jones, an Englishman grateful for his
material success, hardly whipped his native land with anything more damaging
than a soft-leaded pencil.

MARK SAMUELS LASNER COLLECTION

Program for *The New Woman*
by Sydney Grundy,
produced at the Comedy Theatre, [1894].

Throughout the late-Victorian period, it was possible—just as it is today—to make a living out of nothing more than an interest in poking fun at feminists. In the 1890s in particular, visual and verbal caricatures of the "New Woman"—the educated, middle-class figure who incarnated England's flourishing women's rights movement—abounded in the periodical press and on the stage. Some of these misogynist satires were crude and quickly forgotten; others, such as Sydney Grundy's melodramatic comedy *The New Woman,* which opened on 1 September 1894, were surprisingly sophisticated and even entertaining (though they could hardly have pleased the women they ridiculed).

Sydney Grundy (1848–1914) focused his attack not so much on the "rebellious" woman in general as on the woman author in particular. In his view, she was a mass of contradictions, preaching against men and marriage, while apt to use her writing as a tool to seduce unsuspecting women's husbands. At the same time, Grundy's play blamed "effeminate" men for encouraging these unnatural new creatures and preferring them to their old-fashioned, unintellectual wives.

Albert Morrow
Poster for *The New Woman*
by Sydney Grundy, produced at the Comedy Theatre, [1894].
Color lithograph, [1897]. [PLATE II]

When spectators saw the poster that Albert Morrow (1863–1927) created to advertise Sydney Grundy's *The New Woman,* they knew that they were looking not at a generalized satirical image, but at a caricature—that is, at a comical representation of an actual person. The figure in question was Mary Chavelita Dunne (1859–1945), who, as "George Egerton," had published a volume of short stories titled *Keynotes* (1893) that shocked the reading public with its bold descriptions of middle-class women characters' erotic desires and sometimes lawless conduct. Audiences knew that Morrow had this female "George" in mind. They recognized the allusion to the key which Aubrey Beardsley had designed for the volume of stories published by Elkin Mathews and John Lane at the Bodley Head. Many readers of *Punch,* too, already had laughed over another recent caricature (called *Donna Quixote*) of thr same author in that magazine's 28 April 1894 issue. Finding herself quite literally the poster-girl for feminism and the preferred object of ridicule for illustrators and cartoonists did not sit well with "George Egerton." In response, she would disavow any connection with the "New Woman" and claim that she was merely a realist, not a writer with a political agenda. Later in her career, moreover—and after her marriage to a theatrical agent, Reginald Golding Bright—she would abandon fiction and write plays for the London stage, choosing in several of these to make fun herself of militant women.

The version of Morrow's poster shown here was printed by David Allen and Sons, Belfast, for *Les Maîtres de l'Affiche,* probably in 1897. Originally, the poster was issued in a larger size to announce the 1894 production of Grundy's play.

Arthur W. Pinero
The Second Mrs. Tanqueray: An Original Play in Four Acts.
London: Printed by J. Miles, 1892.

Could a so-called "fallen woman"—that is, one who had sex outside of marriage—
ever find her way back into Society (with a capital "S") again? Oscar Wilde asked
that very question in 1892, through his play *Lady Windermere's Fan,* and decided
that the answer was a qualified "yes." He allowed Mrs. Erlynne, a woman who had
left her husband and child years earlier for another man, to return to London with a
new identity and once again to find herself sought out and even courted. Yet, after
having this "bad" woman rescue her grown daughter's reputation and thus prove
herself a "good" woman, Wilde sent her and her new husband away, out of England and out of society's view, in a kind of happy exile. Wilde's audiences were not
quite ready to see a female stage character (however much a lady) who had "sinned"
being fully restored to the same social position as her "pure" sisters.

Theatregoers proved that their opinions on this issue were still deeply conservative by flocking to *The Second Mrs. Tanqueray* by Arthur Wing Pinero (1855–1934),
which used the "fallen woman" theme not for comedy, but for melodrama. Pinero's
play ended with the "good" young stepdaughter castigating herself for her lack of
mercy to her formerly "bad" stepmother, and with the male protagonist, Aubrey
Tanqueray, cursing all men who carelessly ruin women, rather than blaming the
women who err. But their change of heart comes too late to save the new wife of
the title, who has already killed herself. Thus this "problem play" allowed mainstream audiences to contemplate the issue of whether social mores were unjust to
women, at the same time that it gave them the reassurance they wanted, by leaving
the "guilty" woman safely dead. This prompt copy for *The Second Mrs. Tanqueray,*
which opened on 27 May 1893, is inscribed by Pinero to Justin Huntly McCarthy
(1830–1912), the Irish politician and novelist.

MARK SAMUELS LASNER COLLECTION

Reviewing for *The World* the performance of Mrs. Patrick Campbell (1865–1940) — who was born Beatrice Stella Tanner — in her role of a lifetime as Paula Tanqueray, William Archer wrote admiringly, "Never was there a more uncompromisingly artistic piece of acting. It was incarnate reality, the haggard truth." The word "haggard" was carefully chosen, for the actress who shot to fame as the protagonist of Pinero's play, when it opened in May 1893 at the St. James's Theatre where George Alexander was actor-manager, represented a new kind of stage femininity. Hers was not the fresh and robust aspect of the conventional Victorian theatrical beauty. With her almost emaciated slenderness, hollow cheeks, and heavily shadowed eyes, she seemed instead to embody the spirit that Walter Pater had described in his 1873 aesthetic meditation on Leonardo Da Vinci's *Mona Lisa*:

> Hers is the head upon which all 'the ends of the world are come,' and the eyelids are a little weary. . . . It is a beauty . . . into which the soul with all its maladies has passed! . . . . She is older than the rocks among which she sits; like the vampire, she has been dead many times, and learned the secrets of the grave. . . .

Certainly, that was how Aubrey Beardsley depicted her in his *Portrait of Mrs. Patrick Campbell,* a stark pen-and-ink drawing for the first issue of *The Yellow Book* in April 1894. Seen in profile, with her waist scarcely wider than her elbow and her fragile head, weighed down by its jet-black hair, drooping forward, she looked rather like a tall wax taper about to melt and collapse.

111. Aubrey Beardsley, Poster for *A Comedy of Sighs* by John Todhunter and *The Land of Heart's Desire* by W.B. Yeats, color lithograph, 1894.

IV. *Studio Scene from "Trilby,"* toy theatre, color lithograph, 1896.

Mrs. Patrick Campbell and Mr. George Alexander in "The Second Mrs. Tanqueray,"
photograph, [1893].

W.S. Penley Charley's Aunt, postcard photograph, [ca. late 1890s].

W.S. Penley Charley's Aunt.
Postcard photograph by T.C. Turner, Rotary Photographic Co., London, [ca. late 1890s].

"Cross-dressing was a regular feature in the music-hall repertory, where it was used for comic effect and often tied to criticism of the upper classes by those below. It also became a staple of the late-Victorian "High Art" stage, taking the form of male impersonation in plays by Shakespeare and in operas by Mozart. Brandon Thomas (1856–1914), a music-hall singer turned legitimate actor and playwright, brought female impersonation to the Royalty Theatre in Soho and created a long-running hit. His farce, *Charley's Aunt*, which opened in December 1892 with the actor-manager William Sydney Penley (1852–1912) in the lead, offered mainstream audiences light relief from the spate of "problem" dramas focused on gender roles by Pinero, Jones, Wilde, and others that dominated the London theatre of the mid-Nineties. *Charley's Aunt* instead played the subject of gender stereotypes strictly for laughs."

MARK SAMUELS LASNER COLLECTION

Aubrey Beardsley
Poster for *A Comedy of Sighs* by John Todhunter and *The Land of Heart's Desire* by
W. B. Yeats, produced at the Avenue Theatre, 29 March 1894.
Color lithograph, 1894. [PLATE III]

Had he lived, there is no doubt that Aubrey Beardsley (1872–98) would have turned
to designing sets and perhaps even costumes for the theatre. His fascination with all
aspects of the London stage was total. In his pen-and-ink drawings from 1894 to
1895 for the art-and-literature quarterly *The Yellow Book,* he repeatedly depicted theatrical subjects. These included portraits of actresses such as Mrs. Patrick Campbell
(1865–1940) and Winifred Emery (1862–1924), as well as views of fashionable audiences, seen in *The Wagnerites* for the October 1894 number of John Lane's magazine. At the same time, Beardsley was also creating book designs and title-pages for
Lane's series of avant-garde fiction. Among those "Keynotes Series" volumes was
the 1894 novel *The Dancing Faun,* by Florence Farr (1860–1917).

Farr, an actress as well as a writer, had already appeared in Ibsen's *Rosmersholm*
(1891) and in G. B. Shaw's *Widowers' Houses* (1892) by the time she began directing
and producing. Although born in Kent, she was a passionate advocate of the new
Irish drama and a yet more passionate friend of both Shaw and, later, of W. B. Yeats
(1865–1939). She shared her devotion to Yeats with Annie Horniman (1860–1937),
who served unofficially as Yeats's secretary and who backed Farr financially in producing *The Land of Heart's Desire* at the Avenue Theatre, the work which introduced him to London as a playwright.

MARK SAMUELS LASNER COLLECTION

ARS POSTERA.

"Venus Domina."

Mr. Aubrey Beer de
Beers,
You're getting quite
a high renown;
Your Comedy of Leers,
you know,
Is posted all about the
town;
This sort of stuff I can-
not puff,
As Boston says, it
makes me "tired";
Your Japanee-Rossetti
girl
Is not a thing to be
desired.

Mr. Aubrey Beer de
Beers,
New English Art (ex-
cuse the chaff)
Is like the Newest Hu-
mour style,
It's not a thing at
which to laugh;

But all the same, you need not maim
   A beauty reared on Nature's rules;
A simple maid *au naturel*
   Is worth a dozen spotted ghouls.

Mr. Aubrey Beer de Beers,
   You put strange phantoms on our walls
If not so daring as *To-day's*,
   Nor quite so Hardy as *St. Paul's*;
Her sidelong eyes, her giddy guise,—
   Grande Dame Sans Merci she may be;
But there is that about her throat
   Which I myself don't care to see.

Mr. Aubrey Beer de Beers,
   The Philistines across the way,
They say her lips—well, never mind
   Precisely what it is they say;
But I have heard a drastic word
   That scarce is fit for dainty ears;
But then their taste is not the kind
   Of taste to flatter Beer de Beers.

Bless me, Aubrey Beer de Beers,
   On fair Elysian lawns apart
Burd Helen of the Trojan time
   Smiles at the latest mode of Art;
Howe'er it be, it seems to me,
   It's not important to be New;
New Art would better Nature's best,
   But Nature knows a thing or two.

Aubrey, Aubrey Beer de Beers,
   Are there no models at your gate,
Live, shapely, possible and clean?
   Or won't they do to "decorate"?
Then by all means bestrew your scenes
   With half the lotuses that blow,
Pothooks and fishing-lines and things,
   But let the human woman go!

BEFORE SUPPER.

Slow, dignified dancing, a decorous
   sight,
Prevails before supper, when people are
   cool;
The accurate Lancers, infallibly right,
   The waltz, grave and stately—no play-
      ing the fool,
            As does Toole.

Then elderly charmers, still trusting to
   chance
To bring them all partners, compla-
   cently wait
For elegant gentlemen eager to dance—
   Not Tooles, rather Irvings, grand,
      graceful, grave, great,
            And sedate.

AFTER SUPPER.

When supper is over frigidity goes,
   Frivolity comes—now for playing the
      fool!
In Lancers linked lines dart regardless of
   toes,
   In vigorous barn dance they caper, for
      who'll
            Now be cool?

The sad, weary wallflowers watch with
   dazed eyes
Such dancing as they have, no doubt,
   never done.
What matter if they should evince some
   surprise?
When supper is over the best of the
   fun   Has begun.

[Owen Seaman]
"Ars Postera," in *Punch*, 21 April 1894.

As always, *Punch* spoke for the middle-class, mainstream male reader (and theatre-goer) who was either baffled or alarmed by new movements in the visual arts, in literature, in social philosophy, and especially in sexual politics. Writing anonymously, Owen Seaman used Tennyson's poem "Lady Clara Vere de Vere" as a jumping-off point to lampoon the theatrical poster art of "Mr. Aubrey Beer de Beers"—i.e., Aubrey Beardsley—and, at the same time, to mock Beardsley's vision of womanhood as "not a thing to be desired." Seaman (1861–1936), a Professor of Literature and Classics at Durham College, Newcastle, and also a compulsive parodist, would later become the editor of *Punch*.

William Rothenstein
The Building of Her Majesty's Theatre.
Pencil, ink, and watercolor, 1897.

Although Max Beerbohm would soon become an influential drama critic at *The Saturday Review,* his theatrical instincts were not always unerring. While visiting New York in 1895, he saw an adaptation of George du Maurier's novel *Trilby* by the American playwright Paul Potter and reported to his half-brother, the actor-manager Herbert Beerbohm Tree, that he was not impressed. Fortunately Tree, who was also there on tour, decided to see the play himself. Immediately recognizing its commercial potential, he purchased the rights at once. The result was one of the biggest London hits of the 1890s. So lucrative a vehicle did it prove, in its 1895 production at the Haymarket, that the profits from it allowed Tree to begin constructing a new theatre, Her Majesty's, which opened its doors in 1897. Shown here is a drawing of what we might call The House That *Trilby* Built, by Sir William Rothenstein (1872–1945), who numbered among Max Beerbohm's closest friends. Like Beerbohm, Aubrey Beardsley, Walter Sickert, and other *Yellow Book* circle artists, Rothenstein believed that the supposedly "low" world of the popular theatre was a fitting subject for "High Art" representations.

MARK SAMUELS LASNER COLLECTION

William Rothenstein, *The Building of Her Majesty's Theatre*,
pencil, ink, and watercolor, 1897.

T. C. Turner, *Miss Dorothea Baird Trilby* and *Mr. Tree Svengali*,
photographs, in *A Souvenir of "Trilby,"* [1895].

[72]

A Souvenir of "Trilby" by Paul M. Potter. Founded on George Du Maurier's Novel Produced for the First Time in London at the Theatre Royal, Haymarket, on the 30th October 1895 by Herbert Beerbohm Tree.
[London: John Walker, 1895].

Henry Irving's revivals of *The Merchant of Venice* brought to late-Victorian audiences a Shylock who was a tragic figure. Yet even as they embraced Irving in the role (knowing that the actor was not a Jew himself), this noble character did not the represent the so-called "Jewish race" as they wanted to see it portrayed onstage. For an image that would confirm the distrust they already felt toward a group increasingly populous in London's East End, they turned to the anti-hero of *Trilby*. The diabolical Svengali, who wields terrifying power over a hapless Christian beauty, became the archetype of Jewish masculinity at its most sinister and fearsome.

But the anti-Semitism of England's theatregoers was only one factor in the craze for *Trilby* and for *Trilby*-related merchandise, such as this handsome souvenir publication. Herbert Beerbohm Tree's production offered another potent lure: the titillation of seeing the lovely Dorothy Baird's naked feet. The spectacle of an actress's bare feet on the West End stage was utterly shocking (almost as shocking as the sight of women's bare armpits, a feature in the most daring of the music hall shows). Baird's role, too—a variation on the whore with a heart of gold—allowed audiences to wax sentimental over a "low" woman, a Parisian artist's model, yet to see this social outcast safely removed from the scene by death. *Trilby* proved a boon not only to the finances of Tree, but to the stage reputation of Dorothea Baird (1875–1933), who was then an unknown twenty-year-old. A year after her role as the model-turned-singer by mesmerism, she married H.B. Irving, the son of Henry Irving, and thus entered the family circle of an actor-manager every bit as hypnotic and despotic as Svengali.

MARK SAMUELS LASNER COLLECTION

Studio Scene from "Trilby."
Toy theatre, issued as art supplement to *The Pittsburgh Dispatch,* 14 June 1896.
Color lithograph by Donaldson Brothers, New York, 1896. [PLATE IV]

Trilby, Paul Potter's adaptation of George du Maurier's 1894 novel, was produced first in America, before it was bought by Herbert Beerbohm Tree and transferred to the London stage. A smashing success with the public, *Trilby* spawned souvenir merchandise on both sides of the Atlantic including this "toy theatre," which recreates the stage set representing the Parisian artist's studio of "Little Billee." The craze for toy theatres—printed sheets intended for children, but often collected by adults—began early in the nineteenth century and continued unbroken into the twentieth. Ironically, such faithful depictions of sets, costumes, and the figures of actors and actresses brought the glamorous stage world into respectable middle-class homes (and into the everyday lives of impressionable children. both male and female), at a time when theatres were still looked upon with suspicion as places that promoted vice.

MARK SAMUELS LASNER COLLECTION

John Hassall
Poster for *The Wild Rabbit* by George Arliss,
produced at the Criterion Theatre, [1899].
Color lithograph, [1899]. [PLATE V]

With his memoir *Up the Years from Bloomsbury* (1927), the actor and playwright
George Arliss (1868–1946) emphasized his solidly middle-class background by
highlighting in the title his Bloomsbury origins. Even though Henry Irving, a successful social climber who mixed with royalty, would eventually help to make the
acting profession more respectable (especially after his knighthood in 1895), any
man who chose to go on the stage when Arliss did, in the 1880s, was commonly assumed to be "low," immoral, and possibly even criminal in his tendencies. Arliss's
memoir records the consternation of his parents at his choice of career and the part-
ing words of his mother, who

> made me promise that I would always wash myself thoroughly before leaving the the-
> atre at night; that I would go in clean and leave without a trace of make-up clinging to
> me. I don't know what suggested this to her, for she had never met actors, and could
> not have known through personal observation of the unpleasant habit of some provin-
> cial mummers of carrying the marks of their calling so as to be plainly visible in the
> bright sunshine. I think she must have read about it. But I am grateful to her for that
> admonition.

To bear any evidence of make-up in the streets did more than single out a man as a
performer by profession; it also potentially identified him as a member of the homosexual underworld, which overlapped in many places with that of the stage.

MARK SAMUELS LASNER COLLECTION

Bram Stoker
Personal Reminiscences of Henry Irving.
London: William Heinemann, 1906.

Sir Henry Irving—born John Henry Brodribb (1838–1905)—was the most famous actor-manager of the late-Victorian period, as well as the first English actor to receive a knighthood. An eccentric figure who helped to redefine stage images of masculinity and to eclipse the conventional "haberdasher's dummy" ideal, he made a great celebrity of himself and of his first leading-lady, Ellen Terry. He also helped to spur the popular revival of Shakespeare with his commercially successful stagings at the Lyceum Theatre of plays such as *The Merchant of Venice*. But he became a lightning-rod for controversy, too. To the playwrights, critics, and performers in sympathy with J. T. Grein and the Independent Stage Society, such as Elizabeth Robins and G. B. Shaw, Irving symbolized the increasingly outmoded actor-manager system and its antiquated reliance on star-vehicles drawn from the past. At the same time, a new generation of stage historians, interested in rediscovering the performance practices of the Elizabethans, scoffed at Irving's anachronistic versions of Shakespeare's dramas.

Bram Stoker (1847–1912), the novelist best known for *Dracula* (1897), gave up a post as drama critic for *The Daily Mail* in Dublin to serve for many years both as Irving's secretary and as his second-in-command at the Lyceum Theatre, where he supervised the running of a company of actors which included Ellen Terry. After Irving's death, he commemorated the star with this memoir. Daringly, he chose as the frontispiece for Volume Two (shown here) a portrait of the actor applying make-up—an "unmanly" image which, even more than ten years after the Oscar Wilde trials, still made homophobic English spectators uncomfortable. But arousing this unease would have appealed to the Irish-born Stoker, who was an admirer of Wilde and who had married Florence Balcombe, one of Wilde's great friends from their early days in Dublin. This copy of Stoker's *Personal Reminiscences* is inscribed to Brandon Thomas, the actor and playwright who scored such a hit with the cross-dressing comedy, *Charley's Aunt*.

MARK SAMUELS LASNER COLLECTION

Paul Renouard, *Henry Irving Making Up*,
in Bram Stoker, *Personal Reminiscences of Henry Irving*, 1906.

Miss Jessie Preston, as Robinson Crusoe, at the Grand Theatre, Islington,
in *Pearson's Photographic Portfolio of Footlight Favourites by Eminent Photographers,* [1895].

Pearson's Photographic Portfolio of Footlight Favourites by Eminent Photographers.
London: C. Arthur Pearson, [1895].

From the 1880s onward, technical improvements in the reproduction of photographs revolutionized the world of publishing. Not only books, but newspapers, magazines, and other serial publications took advantage of the new possibilities for capturing the human face and form cheaply and well. Pen-and-ink drawings of popular theatrical figures were soon replaced by black-and-white photographs. These glamorized images—precursors of the "pin-up" and the " 8 × 10 glossy"—fed and also generated the interest of fans, some of whom lived far from London and would never see their idols in the flesh. *Pearson's Photographic Portfolio* contained no text. Issued in thirteen parts, from December 1894 through March 1896, it consisted solely of portraits—headshots, as well as full-length—of both actresses and actors, some of them in costume and others in evening dress.

The relationship between middle-class consumers who could afford these serial installments at sixpence apiece and the subjects of the photographs was complex. Images of "footlight favourites" were highly prized, and the actors and actresses themselves were equally sought after as ornamental guests at social occasions. But even after the turn of the century, a social chasm remained between "respectable" people and performers, who were assumed to be low in breeding and loose in conduct. This was especially true where bourgeois ladies and women of the stage were concerned. Perhaps only in the Suffrage movement was the distinction between these two groups fully erased, for the middle-class feminists who demonstrated in the streets, allowed themselves to be photographed at public rallies, and sometimes appeared on trial in court broke social taboos that enabled them at last to sympathize with and to appreciate their "sisters," who earned their livings through self-display.

MARK SAMUELS LASNER COLLECTION

Mr. George Robey.
Postcard photograph by R. Brown, Philco Publishing Co., London, [ca. 1900].

Well into the twentieth century, women who went on the stage were assumed to be from the poorest social classes and were called little better than prostitutes, whatever their actual origins or conduct. This was especially true for those appearing in the music halls where, as singers and dancers, they were usually presented in costumes that exposed their "limbs" to the gaze of male spectators. But men who became actors or even music hall comedians and singers, though also likely to encounter social prejudice, faced less of a stigma than their female counterparts and often tried to claim the title of being gentlemen.

George Robey (1869–1954), for instance, let the story circulate that he had turned to a music-hall career only after his middle-class family lost its money and thus after his plans to attend Cambridge were dashed. Although he is immortalized on this turn-of-the-century postcard in the part of a little girl, his most famous performances did not involve cross-dressing, but rather the spoofing of great male figures from history. As George Gamble wrote in the volume *The "Halls,"* Robey "encasked the quintessence of imbecility." So popular did he become that he was known as the "Prime Minister of Mirth." He enjoyed a long career that saw him, in 1935, make the transition to Shakespearean theatre with the role of Falstaff in a production of *Henry IV, Part I*—a feat of crossing-over that none of his female peers from the music halls was allowed to accomplish.

v. John Hassall, Poster for *The Wild Rabbit* by George Arliss, color lithograph, [1899].

VI. G.F. [George Frederick] Scotson-Clark, *Marie Lloyd,* in *The "Halls,"* [1899].

Mr. George Robey, postcard photograph, [ca. 1900].

2918 A MISS VESTA TILLEY. ROTARY PHOTO, E.C.

Miss Vesta Tilley.
Postcard photograph by Rotary Photographic Co., London, [1907].

Cross-dressing was a staple of turn-of-the-century London theatre, and no one was better at it or more celebrated for it than Matilda Alice Powles (1864–1952). Under the stage name "Vesta Tilley," she went from success to success, first as a child performer in the provinces and eventually as one of the greatest stars of the London music halls. A comic singer, she created a range of male characters and made a specialty of satirizing military officers. But her most famous stage persona was "Burlington Bertie," a strutting West End dandy and "toff." Her impersonations of gentlemen and her skewerings of their foibles appealed to two audiences simultaneously: male and female theatregoers in the Gallery—working-class people who loved to laugh at their social "betters"—and the aristocratic male patrons in the Boxes and the Orchestra Stalls, who could well afford (in every sense) a little harmless fun at their own expense. The fame of "Miss Vesta Tilley," which overshadowed that of other contemporary female-as-male performers such as Ella Shields and Hetty King, is confirmed by this postcard showing her in three different roles, including that of an elegant and affluent lady. This last, too, was an acted part, for "Vesta Tilley" was no leisured ornament, but a professional woman working constantly at perfecting her craft.

G. F. [George Frederick] Scotson-Clark
The "Halls." Pictures by G. F. Scotson-Clark.
London: T. Fisher Unwin, [1899]. [PLATE VI]

In Emily Morse Symonds's ("George Paston's") 1898 novel, *A Writer of Books,* the upper-middle-class heroine longs to attend a music-hall performance, believing that she must enlarge her range of experience in order to write realistic fiction. But her fiancé refuses her request, saying that such entertainments were unsuitable for ladies, especially innocent and unmarried ones. His opinion was shared by many gentlemen, who chose to keep what were known familiarly as the "Halls" to themselves.

Ironically, ladies did have access to images from the music halls in many forms. Songs from the "Halls" became immensely popular, and sheet music illustrated with drawings or photographs of the female performers who sang them appeared in respectable homes everywhere. Serious artists' books, including G. F. Scotson-Clark's *The "Halls,"* also featured portraits of stars such as Marie Lloyd (1870–1922), who rose from the working classes to the heights of professional success. In his essay for the volume, George Gamble was oddly indifferent to this beloved and celebrated comic singer, dismissing her with a single sentence: "Miss Marie Lloyd I *have* seen; and I am told that *she* is good."

MARK SAMUELS LASNER COLLECTION

Walter Sickert
The Old Oxford Music Hall, in *The Yellow Book: An Illustrated Quarterly,* Volume I,
April 1894.

Music halls were the preferred form of public entertainment for working-class audiences, both male and female, but also for late-Victorian men of the higher classes.
Safe from respectable ladies' disapproval, gentlemen enjoyed the freedom of hearing risqué song lyrics and of ogling chorus girls who danced in shortened skirts and
flesh-colored tights or who posed in living tableaux while wearing body stockings
that gave the illusion of nudity. But the delights that men sought at the "Halls"
were not confined to the stage. In 1894, there was a public outcry to shut down the
Empire Theatre, one of London's most popular music halls, because its promenade
was allegedly the haunt of prostitutes (male, as well as female) who gathered in
search of customers.

   Walter Sickert (1860–1942) was among a growing number of artists—many associated with J.M. Whistler's aesthetic circles or with the French-inspired Decadents—who refused to dismiss music halls as "low" places and who viewed them
instead as subjects worthy of "High Art" treatment. John Lane's avant-garde quarterly of art and literature, *The Yellow Book* (1894–1897) would reproduce several of
Sickert's oils devoted to music-hall stages and audiences. The Oxford (erected in
1861 and rebuilt in 1893), stood at the corner of Oxford Street and Tottenham Court
Road. Although Sickert's painting depicts a characteristic scene with a female performer at center stage, the Oxford was also home to successful male singers and
comics such as George Robey, who made his London debut there in 1891.

Walter Sickert, *The Old Oxford Music Hall*, in *The Yellow Book*, April 1894.

Mrs. Langtry as "Miss Hardcastle," photograph, [1881].

Mrs. Langtry as "Miss Hardcastle."
Photograph by London Stereoscope Company, London, [1881].

For women at the end of the nineteenth century, there were many possible routes to the stage. Some actresses—such as Ellen, Marion, Kate, and Florence Terry—were the daughters of performers and thus in effect merely entered the family business. Some (especially those from working-class backgrounds) chose the theatre as a last resort to save themselves from starvation or prostitution, especially if they had already been "ruined" by men and thus had become unfit for employment as servants in respectable households. A few were educated women who felt a deep interest in public performance and who sought professional training in how to speak and move onstage. (This was true of Eleanor Marx-Aveling, daughter of Karl Marx, who never actually had a stage career, but did take acting lessons.) But others in effect drifted into drama, to capitalize upon their notoriety from some other sphere.

The most famous of all such "accidental" actresses was Lillie Langtry (1853–1929), who was already a celebrated society beauty—and one of the mistresses of the Prince of Wales—when she made her London debut at the Haymarket Theatre in 1881, playing Kate Hardcastle in a production of Oliver Goldsmith's *She Stoops to Conquer*. It was said that Oscar Wilde, her friend and public admirer, was the one who suggested that she support herself by going onstage. This would have been a daring idea indeed and thus likely to have come from the publicity-savvy Wilde, since ladies of her class (however much in need of money) seldom associated with actresses, let alone joined their ranks.

MARK SAMUELS LASNER COLLECTION

Miss Lillah McCarthy, photograph, [1896].

Miss Lillah McCarthy.
Photograph by W. and D. Downey, London, [1896].

Her greatest successes would come in the decade when Edward VII sat on (and sometimes overflowed) the throne—the decade that saw her move from one triumphant experience to another, playing the leads in the first productions of Shaw's major plays, often under the direction of Harley Granville-Barker (whom she married in 1906). But in the 1890s, Lillah McCarthy (1875–1960) scored her first hit in the one-dimensional role of Mercia, the "good" woman in *The Sign of the Cross* (1895), Wilson Barrett's crowd-pleaser about the early Christians martyrs. (She is seen here in a photograph that probably dates from 1896, when she joined Barrett's company.) "Mercia" was a part very different from the complex images of powerful, willful femininity in which she would later specialize. So, too, her early wish to be a star onstage gave little hint of how influential she would later prove behind the scenes, as Granville-Barker's working-partner and collaborator in their many attempts before the start of World War I to turn the Royal Court, then the Savoy and other theatres, into sites where audiences would be stimulated to think and shaken up by the clash of social and political ideas.

MARK SAMUELS LASNER COLLECTION

Boyle Lawrence, ed.
Celebrities of the Stage.
London: George Newnes, [1899–1900]. [PLATE VII]

Although the London theatre world was a major industry in itself, it also fueled and was in turn fueled by a host of associated industries. Among the largest and most lucrative of these was the publishing business. The turn of the century saw a new market for printed versions of hit plays. (And, as Wilde, Shaw, Barrie and others discovered, a playwright who added detailed and discursive stage directions, prefaces, or character analyses that functioned as "extra" information for the purchaser—rather like the "director's commentary" for films on DVD today—could boost the sales of published plays.)

But if consumers seemed interested in owning copies of contemporary plays, they were far more eager to buy images of the stars who made their names in such vehicles, especially when those stars were female and glamorous. With improved technologies for reproducing photographs available, ventures such as *Celebrities of the Stage* appeared and stoked the fires of fandom. Like Pearson's *Footlight Favorites*, Newnes's *Celebrities of the Stage* was issued serially; unlike the former, *Celebrities* offered the bait of full-page images in color. Shown here is the third of twelve parts, open to a heliochrome reproduction of a photograph (by Alfred Ellis) of Evelyn Millard. Accompanying the image is a tribute to the actress—written by Boyle Lawrence in the gushing prose style of theatrical publicity familiar to readers even today—and to her performance in *The Adventure of Lady Rosa*, where hers was a leg-baring "trouser role." As Lawrence says enthusiastically, "Her womanly manliness is irresistible. . . . with such freshness, such girlish impulsiveness." Though this commentary emphasizes the appeal of youth and asserts later that her "years upon the stage are very few," Millard, who was born in 1869, was almost thirty years old at the time she assumed this part. Nonetheless, her looks allowed her to make a specialty of playing ingénues. (In February 1895, she had originated the role of Cecily Cardew in the first production of Wilde's *The Importance of Being Earnest*.)

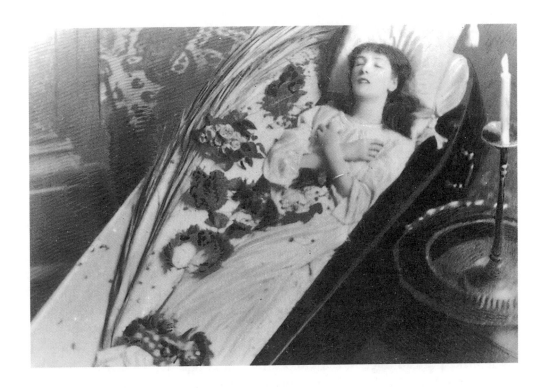

Sarah Bernhardt in Her Coffin.
Photograph, from a private photograph made in the early 1870s, [ca. 1900].

The Divine Sarah was never more divine than when she was playing dead. She not only specialized in roles that allowed her to expire, whether gracefully or wrenchingly, onstage; she liked it to be known that in her private life, too, she was in touch with mortality. Thus she had herself photographed in the coffin in which she reputedly slept. It was no wonder that she remained a favorite of the British male aesthetes and Decadents—including Oscar Wilde and Aubrey Beardsley—throughout the 1880s and 1890s, for they insisted that the greatest forms of beauty must be "strange" and even "morbid." When she crossed the Channel from France for her frequent English tours, they made her the subject of sonnets and of sketches. Indeed, the great Jewish actress was to have been Wilde's Jewish princess, Salome, in 1892, until the Lord Chamberlain's Office denied the play a license and thus stopped a production which would have spotlighted Bernhardt in a new kind of love-death—crushed by soldiers while kissing a severed head.

MARK SAMUELS LASNER COLLECTION

Max Beerbohm
"Hamlet, Princess of Denmark," in *The Saturday Review*, 17 June 1899.

Female Hamlets were nothing new. They dated back to Sarah Siddons in the eighteenth century and were a staple in the repertory of nineteenth-century actresses, such as the American star, Charlotte Cushman. At the same time, "trouser roles" were a regular feature in the career of Sarah Bernhardt (1844–1923), who not only enjoyed a hit in the cross-dressed part of Napoleon's son in Edmond Rostand's *L'Aiglon*, but, more daringly, allowed a photograph to circulate of herself wearing trousers offstage while at work on a sculpture.

Still, it was a newsworthy event when Bernhardt assayed the challenge of *Hamlet*, which she brought to London in a French prose adaptation that was partly the work of Oscar Wilde's friend, the poet Marcel Schwob. (It was Schwob who had helped with matters of style and correctness, when Wilde was writing the play *Salome* in French.) But if Bernhardt's performance marked a historic occasion and histrionic milestone, Max Beerbohm, who had just completed his first year as the drama critic for *The Saturday Review*, insisted that it also proved a risible one. His scathing review began and ended with the assertion that the evening had offered not a Shakespearean tragedy, but a modern comedy and that he had barely managed to keep from laughing. Most ridiculous, from his perspective, was the "absurd" spectacle of an actress as the Danish prince, for despite the character's "feminine qualities," Hamlet was "none the less a man because he is not consistently manly, just as Lady Macbeth is none the less a woman for being a trifle unsexed." (His comments did, of course, conveniently ignore the facts of Elizabethan staging, which would have presented a boy in the latter role.)

MARK SAMUELS LASNER COLLECTION

Pamela Colman Smith
Poster for *Shakespeare's Heroines Calendar 1899*
published by R. H. Russell, New York.
Color lithograph, [1898]. [PLATE VIII]

By the end of the nineteenth century, the Victorian interest in Shakespeare productions (and especially in Shakespearean heroines, as embodied by glamorous actresses) had become a craze. Like all such popular fads, this one, too, inspired the publishing industries both in Britain and in the United States to capitalize on consumer interest. Shown here is what today we might call a "merchandising tie-in"—a poster for a calendar that featured artistic interpretations of the female protagonists from Shakespeare's major plays.

The poster artist was Pamela Colman Smith, born in England to American parents in 1878. (Sources disagree as to the year of her death, which was sometime in the early 1950s.) A true female eccentric with a multitude of talents, she resembled Mabel Dearmer in her willingness to explore a range of careers in both the visual and theatrical worlds of art. She spent her early life in Jamaica, but as an adult moved often between New York and London, where she combined membership in the circle of the Terry family—it was Ellen Terry who supposedly gave her the nickname "Pixie"—with equally close relationships with W. B. Yeats and his artist brother, Jack Yeats. She published many drawings and book illustrations and had work exhibited in galleries at the turn of the century. At the same time, she remained fascinated by the stage and in 1904 appeared in a performance of Yeats's *The Land of Heart's Desire*.

MARK SAMUELS LASNER COLLECTION

E. W. Tarver
Mrs. Langtry as "Rosalind" in "As You Like It" 1890, in *A Chronicle of the St. James's Theatre from its Origin in 1835*.
[London: 1900?].

Ada Rehan as Rosalind.
Photograph by Napoleon Sarony, New York, 1890.

Miss Julia Neilson as "Rosalind" in "As You Like It."
Photograph by Alfred Ellis, London, [1896–98].

Miss Phyllis Dare [as Rosalind].
Postcard photograph by Rotary Photographic Co., London. [ca. 1915].

Shown here are four images of four different actresses (from two generations) who performed Rosalind in *As You Like It* at the turn of the century. The oldest of the four was Lillie Langtry, born in 1853; the youngest was Phyllis Dare (whose real name was the less sensational Phyllis Dones), born in 1890. In between came Ada Rehan (1860–1916), who was renowned for her comic work, and Julia Neilson (1868–1957), whose interpretation of Rosalind in the mid-Nineties was probably the most celebrated.

Why did audiences so love to see their favorite actresses in this part? Certainly, Rosalind was one of Shakespeare's strongest heroines and could be played as a kind of "New Woman"; yet she also remained witty and winsome and, best of all, could be relied upon not to burst into a denunciation of men or of British marriage laws, as contemporary feminist stage characters were wont to do. But the most superficial—and commercial—reason for her appeal involved the opportunity for cross-dressing in a woodland tunic and tights. On the legitimate stage and in a "High Art" setting, audiences could get the *frisson* of seeing a woman's legs, the same pleasure they would otherwise have had to seek in the less respectable music halls.

Mrs. LANGTRY

69

As Rosalind in
"As You Like it"
1890

MISS JULIA NEILSON AS "ROSALIND"
IN "AS YOU LIKE IT."

ALFRED ELLIS

20, UPPER BAKER STREET,
LONDON. N.W.

Four actresses in the role of Rosalind :

E. W. Tarver, *Mrs. Langtry as "Rosalind" in "As You Like It"* 1890,
in *A Chronicle of the St. James's Theatre from its Origin in 1835,* [1900?].

Ada Rehan as Rosalind, photograph, 1890.

Miss Julia Neilson as "Rosalind" in "As You Like It," photograph, [1896–98].

Miss Phyllis Dare [as Rosalind], postcard photograph, [ca. 1915].

[95]

Hugh Beaumont, *Ellen Terry as Portia,* watercolor, [ca. 1897].

VII. *Evelyn Millard,* heliochrome reproduction of photograph by Alfred Ellis, in Boyle Lawrence, ed., *Celebrities of the Stage,* [1899–1900].

VIII. Pamela Colman Smith, Poster for *Shakespeare's Heroines Calendar 1899*, color lithograph, [1898].

Hugh Beaumont
Ellen Terry as Portia.
Watercolor, [ca. 1897]

Trying to conjure up the most outrageously extreme, the very newest "New Woman" that he could, George Bernard Shaw made the character of Vivie Warren in *Mrs. Warren's Profession* (a play written in 1893, but not produced by the Stage Society until 1902) a cigar-smoking graduate of Newnham College with legal ambitions. As she explains matter-of-factly in Act One:

> I shall set up chambers in the City, and work at actuarial calculations and conveyancing. Under cover of that I shall do some law, with one eye on the Stock Exchange all the time. I've come down here by myself to read law: not for a holiday, as my mother imagines.

Mainstream late-Victorian audiences were appalled at the idea of a woman practicing law—unless, that is, the woman in question was the charming Portia. The very same blurring of conventional gender roles and usurping of masculine careers that generated anxiety in modern life could be contemplated lightly and even appreciatively, when represented at a safe remove, through stagings of *The Merchant of Venice*. One of the most celebrated of these was Henry Irving's, which featured Ellen Terry in a newly serious, even solemn interpretation of Shakespeare's cross-dressed heroine, who saves her lover by defending him in court. This watercolor homage to Terry in the role likely dates from the time of Irving's July 1897 production at the Lyceum Theatre, which also cast Terry's daughter, Edith Craig, as Jessica and her son, (Edward) Gordon Craig, as Lorenzo.

MARK SAMUELS LASNER COLLECTION

Souvenir Programme Given by the Theatrical & Musical Professions as a Tribute to Miss Ellen Terry on the Occasion of Her Jubilee, Tuesday Afternoon, June 12th, 1906.
London: Printed and published by J. Miles & Co., 1906.

Although she was only fifty-nine-years-old in 1906, Ellen Terry had indeed been a working professional on the stage for fifty years, having grown up in a theatrical family and made her debut (in Shakespeare's *The Winter's Tale*) at age nine. If any figure of the late-Victorian period embodied the public's idea of The Actress, it was Terry. That she had been so open in her sexual non-conformity—marrying and divorcing several times, as well as living in a "free union" with Edwin Godwin and having two children with him—and yet been able to command the respect and the affection of bourgeois audiences was a tribute to the power of her talents, as well a harbinger of changing social mores (or at least a sign that the public was willing to grant "show people" special latitude and expected no better of women who went on the stage).

The six-hour-long celebration of Ellen Terry's career at the Drury Lane Theatre Royal—called a "Golden Jubilee," to echo the festivities of the late 1880s held in honor of Queen Victoria and thus to honor Terry as the London theatre's equivalent of a female monarch—was not originally scheduled as a tribute to her alone. It was to have paid homage to Sir Henry Irving, as well. But Irving's death the year before turned the occasion into one dedicated to Terry. Yet, if this new focus confirmed the supremacy of women in the theatre, the backstage organization of it suggested otherwise. Not only was the Executive Committee put in charge of arrangements chaired by a man (the playwright Arthur Wing Pinero), but no woman was invited to participate in either of the two committees planning the daylong events or indeed to have a major role onstage. Leading actresses of the day who wished to join in were relegated to being silent props in a *tableau*—a decision which so shocked Terry that she suggested to Pinero that perhaps she should have appeared only in the *tableau* herself. As it was, she concluded this "Jubilee" by proving that a professional actress's work was never done, hurrying from the site of the festivities to the Court Theatre, where she performed as usual that evening in *Captain Brassbound's Conversion*, in a part which G. B. Shaw had written for her.

Souvenir Programme Given by the Theatrical & Musical Professions as a Tribute to Miss Ellen Terry on the Occasion of Her Jubilee, Tuesday Afternoon, June 12th, 1906.

William Nicholson, *Souvenir Scroll for the Ellen Terry Commemoration Banquet,* color lithograph, [1906].

William Nicholson
Souvenir Scroll for the Ellen Terry Commemoration Banquet.
Color lithograph, [1906].

The "Ellen Terry Golden Jubilee" was indeed a landmark. It not only honored Terry herself but, by extension, the notion of working women as admirable and influential figures, potentially every bit as important as the late Queen, who in 1887 and in 1897 had been celebrated with two jubilee spectacles. The event served, moreover, as confirmation that stage-acting, which formerly ranked as a lowly trade, could now be acknowledged as a profession and an art, even when practiced by a woman. The prominent role of "true" artists—that is, of male visual artists—in the commemoration clearly was meant to indicate that they recognized Terry as an equal. Thus the cover for the souvenir program was designed by William Nicholson, the title-page was provided by Walter Crane, and the program itself contained depictions of Terry in her greatest roles in plates by Edwin Austin Abbey, William Orpen, Byam Shaw, John Singer Sargent, James Pryde, Lawrence Alma-Tadema, Bernard Partridge, and Nicholson.

It was William Nicholson (1872–1949), too, the painter and printmaker who had designed the sets for Barrie's *Peter Pan* in 1904, who also created this remarkable "souvenir scroll" with representations of Terry in her major roles. The illustrated scroll was distributed to guests at the dinner held in Terry's honor five days after the matinee performance, on 17 June 1906 at the Hotel Cecil.

No. 190ᴳ J.B.&Cᵒ.   MISS ELLEN TERRY   WINDOW & GROVE.

Program for *Miss Ellen Terry Recital.*
London, [1912].

Although one of her greatest stage successes came in a non-Shakespearean role, as the eponymous heroine of *Olivia* (1878), based on Goldsmith's *The Vicar of Wakefield*, Ellen Terry was most closely identified with the wide range of Shakespeare's women from Ophelia to Lady Macbeth. It was, therefore, only fitting that she would choose in the latter part of her career to tour in a one-woman show which allowed her both to lecture on Shakespeare's female characters and to offer demonstrations of "illustrative acting."

MARK SAMUELS LASNER COLLECTION

The Women's Exhibition 1909.
London: The Women's Press, 1909.

Whether radicals or reformers, turn-of-the-century activists in the British suffrage movements all agreed that theatre could be a potent weapon in their struggles. It could cheer and divert fellow suffragists, as did the charming one-act farce *How the Vote Was Won* by Cicely Hamilton and Christopher St John [Christabel Marshall]. It could reach and persuade audiences that might otherwise be indifferent to the cause or ignorant of its logic. And it could also serve as an effective means of fund-raising. Because so many professional actresses endorsed the call for women's suf-frage—they were, after all, workers and taxpayers who understood why they deserved political representation—the quality of benefit performances could often be quite high.

This program for the 1909 "Women's Exhibition" staged by the National Women's Social and Political Union trumpets (quite literally) the "splendid enter-tainments" provided with the "generous help of the Actresses' Franchise League and their friends." These included theatrical sketches written by the likes of Anthony Hope (author of *The Prisoner of Zenda*) and starring such notables of the British theatre as Lillah McCarthy and Lilian Braithwaite (1873–1948), who began her London stage career in 1897 as Celia opposite Julia Neilson's Rosalind in *As You Like It* and would go on later to star in Noël Coward's successful melodrama, *The Vortex* (1924).

The cover for this program was designed by (Estelle) Sylvia Pankhurst (1882–1960), the socialist and suffragist leader who was daughter to Emmeline Pankhurst and sister to Christabel. Before devoting herself to political activism, she studied at the Manchester Municipal School of Art and the Royal College of Art.

The National Women's Social & Political Union

4, Clement's Inn, London.

The Women's Exhibition 1909

Prince's Skating Rink
Knightsbridge **London**

May 13th to 26th

Programme
Price 3D

The Woman's Press,
4, Clement's Inn, London, W.C.

The Women's Exhibition 1909, 1909.

Mr. Lewis Sydney Suffragette Maud Allan, pencil, ink, and watercolor, [1910–1911].

Mr. Lewis Sydney Suffragette Maud Allan.
Pencil, ink, and watercolor, [1910–1911].

The "revue" was a new mode of stage entertainment, introduced to London at the end of the nineteenth century and reaching its peak of popularity around the time of World War I. It was closely related in form to the programs of the music halls, combining a group of unrelated sketches, as well as both music and comedy; it differed, however, in featuring a cast that appeared in various roles throughout the evening, rather than a succession of performers each doing a single "turn." Like the music hall shows, though, many of the revues were notable for promoting the chance to see beautiful women in glamorous, skin-baring costumes.

One of the best-known examples of the revue was the series of "Follies" produced by H.G. Pélissier (1874–1913) at the Apollo Theatre in Shaftesbury Avenue from 1908 to 1912. These shows often spotlighted the attractive young Fay Compton (1894–1978), who became Pélissier's wife and who went on later to a long and distinguished career in serious theatre. (She would enjoy one of her final successes in a 1959 production at the Old Vic of Wilde's *The Importance of Being Earnest.*)

Like the music halls, the revues might have been daring in their exposure of women's bodies, but they were often conservative in their social attitudes, especially where gender was concerned. Shown here is the costume design, probably by the theatrical costuming firm of B.J. Simmons and Co., for a cross-dressed take-off called "Burlesque of a Maud Allan Matinee," which was part of the program for Pélissier's "Follies" of 1911. There were two obvious targets for ridicule in Lewis Sydney's performance: One was the dancer Maud Allan, who continued to revive her 1908 piece inspired by Oscar Wilde's character, *The Vision of Salome.* But the other object of laughter was the suffragette—a woman such as Emmeline, Sylvia, or Christabel Pankhurst, who was willing to engage in civil disobedience and be dragged away to prison in manacles for her beliefs.

MARK SAMUELS LASNER COLLECTION

Program for *Votes for Women! A Dramatic Tract in Three Acts*
by Elizabeth Robins,
produced at the Royal Court Theatre, [1907].

In 1907, the Lord Chamberlain's Office refused to license Harley Granville-Barker's play, *Waste,* because of its open use of a situation related to abortion. But that same year, Granville-Barker also produced at the Royal Court Theatre a drama that spoke of abortion, this time more discreetly and ambiguously in the context of the "Woman Question" in general, without encountering censorship. Elizabeth Robins's *Votes for Women!* opened on 9 April 1907, the exclamation in its title announcing that this was no mere evening's entertainment, but a piece of advocacy and a cry for political action. As the subtitle declaring the play a "tract" suggested, Elizabeth Robins, who had cut her teeth both as an actress and as a producer in the 1890s with the first English stagings of several works by Ibsen, saw the potential for fusing polemics with theatrical effects. Act Two daringly erased the distinction between stage and street, and between artificial and actual spectacle. It opened in Trafalgar Square and reproduced the dynamics of a public rally by suffrage leaders, with working-class and middle-class female characters delivering speeches identical to those that could be heard by anyone who might attend such open-air meetings. The play's heroine is a "fallen" woman who has made her way back into Society (with, as in Wilde's and Pinero's plays of the Nineties, a capital "S"), in order to spread feminist activism among the educated classes. She describes the "greatest evil in the world" as the "helplessness of women." But Elizabeth Robins herself was the antithesis of "helpless." Robins became a key member of several suffrage organizations, including the Women's Social and Political Union, the Actresses' Franchise League, and the Women Writers' Suffrage League. Around this time, she also turned from involvements with men to form a lasting partnership with Dr. Octavia Wilberforce (1888–1963), the medical reformer.

MARK SAMUELS LASNER COLLECTION

FOR TWO WEEKS ONLY,

EVERY EVENING at 8.30,

Last Matinee, Wednesday, May 22nd, at 2.30,

Votes for Women!

A Dramatic Tract in Three Acts,
By ELIZABETH ROBINS.

Lord John Wynnstay	...	Mr. ATHOL FORDE
The Hon. Geoffrey Stonor	...	Mr. AUBREY SMITH
Mr. St. John Greatorex	...	*Mr. E. HOLMAN CLARK
Mr. Richard Farnborough	...	Mr. P. CLAYTON GREENE
Mr. Freddy Tunbridge	...	Mr. PERCY MARMONT
Mr. Allen Trent	...	Mr. LEWIS CASSON
Mr. Walker	...	Mr. EDMUND GWENN
Lady John Wynnstay	...	Miss MAUD MILTON
Mrs. Heriot	...	Miss FRANCES IVOR
Miss Vida Levering	...	Miss WYNNE MATTHISON
Miss Beatrice Dunbarton	...	Miss JEAN MacKINLAY
Mrs. Freddy Tunbridge	...	Miss GERTRUDE BURNETT
Miss Ernestine Blunt	...	Miss DOROTHY MINTO
A Working Woman	...	Miss AGNES THOMAS

*The Management is indebted to Mr. Frederick Harrison for allowing Mr. E. Holman Clark to appear.

Act I.	-	Wynnstay House in Hertfordshire.
Act II.	-	Trafalgar Square, London.
Act III.	-	Eaton Square, London.

The Entire Action of the Play takes place between Sunday noon and six o'clock in the evening of the same day.

There will be Intervals of 15 Minutes between the Acts.

PROGRAMME OF MUSIC.

1. OUVERTURE	...	"Le pré aux clercs"	...	Herold
2. SYMPHONY No. 2 in D major (Scherzo and Finale)	...			Beethoven
3. (a) MELODY in F major	...	...	...	Rubenstein
(b) MOMENT MUSICAL, Op. 94, No. 2	...	...		Schubert
(c) VALSE, Op. 48	...	...	...	Tschaikowsky

Last Matinee, Wednesday, May 22nd at 2.30.

Opera Glasses, by Negretti & Zambra, can be obtained from the Attendants, price 6d.

Prices of Admission : Private Boxes, £2 2s. and £3 3s. Stalls, 10s. 6d.
Dress Circle, 7s. 6d. and 5s. Upper Circle, 4s. Pit, 2s. 6d. Gallery, 1s.

Doors Open at 8. Matinees at 2.

BOX OFFICE (Mr. H. P. Towers) OPEN 10 to 10.

Telephone 48 Westminster

NO FEES.

The Management beg to announce that the Refreshment Bars are under their sole control, and all Wines, Spirits, Tea and Coffee are of the best quality.

Extracts from the Rules made by the London County Council.—The name of the actual and responsible Manager of the Theatre must be printed on every play bill. The Public can leave the Theatre at the end of the Performance by all exit and entrance doors, which must open outwards.

Where there is a fireproof screen to the proscenium opening, it must be lowered at least once during every performance to ensure its being in proper working order. Smoking is not permitted in the auditorium. All Gangways, passages and staircases must be kept free from chairs or any other obstructions, whether permanent or temporary

Stage Manager	...	Mr. WILFRID FRANKS
Musical Director	...	Mr. THEODORE STIER
Business Manager	...	Mr. E. TAYLOR PLATT

The Last Performance of the Season will take place on Saturday, June 29th next.
The Vedrenne-Barker Performances will be resumed on Monday, September 16th, 1907, at the Savoy Theatre.

Program for *Votes for Women!* by Elizabeth Robins, [1907].

[107]

Max Beerbohm, *Mr. Stanley Houghton*, pencil, ink, and watercolor, [ca. 1912–1913].

Max Beerbohm
Mr. Stanley Houghton.
Pencil, ink, and watercolor, [ca. 1912–1913].

In 1910, after twelve years as the drama critic for *The Saturday Review*, Max Beer-bohm gave up that choice position. But he never gave up his interest in contemporary theatre or his urge to comment acidly upon the figures who populated it. Often, he used the latter impulse to spur his visual caricaturing, as in this group lampoon of the major Edwardian dramatists. The "new boy" here is Stanley Houghton (1881–1913), a Manchester-born playwright influenced by Ibsen's "problem plays," who had made a splash in 1912 with the London production of his *Hindle Wakes.* He is welcomed here into the company of such younger and older theatrical stalwarts as J.M. Barrie, Arthur Wing Pinero, John Masefield, Harley Granville-Barker, George Bernard Shaw, John Galsworthy, Henry Arthur Jones, and Alfred Sutro.

Tellingly, Beerbohm—who preferred women to charm him as pretty and girlish figures onstage—chose to make this an all-boys' gathering. Had he wished, though, he might well have placed Houghton alongside Ibsen-admiring women playwrights such as Elizabeth Robins or Cicely Hamilton (1872–1952), whose *Diana of Dobson's* had enjoyed success in 1908 at the Kingsway Theatre, where it was produced by and starred the female actor-manager, Lena Ashwell (1872–1957).

MARK SAMUELS LASNER COLLECTION

Laurence Housman
Max.
Ink, [ca. 1900–1905].

At the turn of the century, an appointment as the drama critic for one of England's major newspapers or magazines required no special training in stagecraft and no experience with acting or with writing for the theatre. It did not even demand higher education, for some critics had a university background and others did not. All one needed was to be able to write quickly, pointedly, and wittily and to be male. Although women journalists filled a variety of roles, none of the major dailies, weeklies, or monthlies based in London employed a woman as a regular reviewer of plays.

When Max Beerbohm (1872–1956) succeeded G.B. Shaw as the drama critic at *The Saturday Review* in 1898, his chief theatrical credential was an accident of birth, for he was half-brother to the actor-manager Herbert Beerbohm Tree (1853–1917). A mere twenty-six-years-old, he had made his name largely through his writings for *The Yellow Book,* one volume of comical literary sketches in 1896, and another of visual lampoons of celebrities, called *Caricatures of Twenty-Five Gentlemen* (1896). But for several years he had been an almost obsessive theatregoer, as well as a reserved, diffident version of a "stage-door Johnny," whose infatuations with actresses were realized mainly in print. Two years after becoming a professional reviewer, however, he also entered the London theatre world as a playwright, adapting his short story "The Happy Hypocrite" for a production at the Royalty Theatre in 1900. Beerbohm is depicted here, around the time of his dual success as a writer about and a writer for the stage, in a caricature sketch by Laurence Housman (1865–1959). Housman—younger brother of the poet A.E. Housman—was another figure of multiple talents, who illustrated books and also wrote novels and plays.

LAURENCE HOUSMAN PAPERS, SEYMOUR ADELMAN COLLECTION, BRYN MAWR COLLEGE LIBRARY

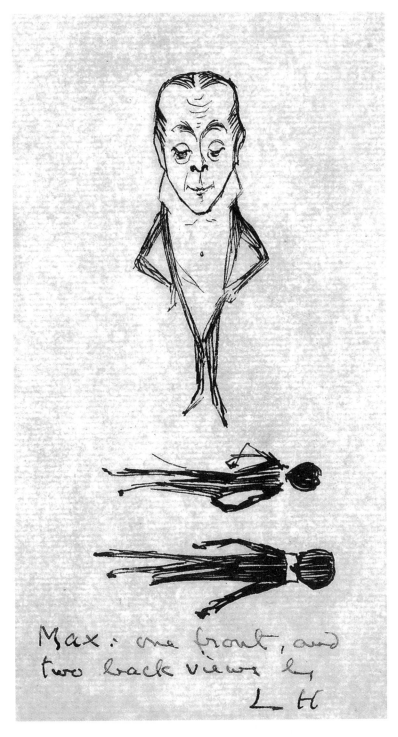

Laurence Housman, *Max,* ink, [ca. 1900–1905].

Laurence Housman
Self-portrait.
Ink, [ca. 1900–1904].

It was hardly surprising that Laurence Housman, who contributed two startlingly homoerotic drawings to *The Yellow Book* in the mid-1890s, would eventually be attracted to the world of the theatre. Even before his *Bethlehem* premiered onstage in 1902 (in a production directed by Edward Gordon Craig, the son of Ellen Terry), he had shown an interest in impersonation and writing "in character." In 1900, he enjoyed large sales and excellent reviews for *An Englishwoman's Love Letters,* a first-person epistolary novel which he published anonymously and which most readers assumed to have been penned by a female author. This sustained exercise certainly gave him practice at creating a woman's voice and at representing women's emotions from the inside. Such experience would prove valuable much later in life, when he wrote his biggest stage hit, *Victoria Regina,* a drama about the woman who had been Queen in his youth. It opened to acclaim in 1935 on Broadway, where it proved one of Helen Hayes's best roles, and later was brought to London.

Laurence Housman
Sex and the Censorship.
Autograph manuscript, [1928?].

Fear of censorship dogged British playwrights throughout the period of 1880–1920. The Lord Chamberlain's Office had the power to refuse licenses necessary for public performance on a variety of grounds. It could, of course, do so with plays considered indecent or shocking in their content or language. But it could also withhold its approval from any theatrical work which dramatized a Biblical story or depicted English royalty. Mabel Dearmer, the artist and writer, ran up against the prejudices of the Lord Chamberlain's Office with her seemingly harmless attempts at producing Christian Mystery plays. So, too, did the illustrator and author Laurence Housman, who claimed that fully thirty-two of his works intended for the turn-of-the-century stage had been embroiled in controversy or banned for one paltry reason or another. In the manuscript of "Sex and the Censorship," his retrospective meditation upon the topic composed in the late 1920s, Housman likened the experiences of several of his (lesser-known) plays, to the fates of Ibsen's *Ghosts,* Shaw's *Mrs. Warren's Profession,* Harley Granville-Barker's *Waste,* and even to so late a work as Radclyffe Hall's 1928 lesbian novel, *The Well of Loneliness,* which was banned as an "obscene libel." "Sex," he concluded wearily, "is still a tribal taboo."

LAURENCE HOUSMAN PAPERS, SEYMOUR ADELMAN COLLECTION, BRYN MAWR COLLEGE LIBRARY

Jane Emmet de Glehn
Harley Granville-Barker.
Pencil, 1912.

Along with his friend and close associate, G.B. Shaw, Harley Granville-Barker (1877–1946) picked up the mantle dropped by the groundbreaking producers of Ibsen's works in the late 1880s and early 1890s. During the first decade of the twentieth century, he became the center of the new movement to turn the London stage into a place where social and political ideas, including those focused on women's rights and roles, could be debated openly.

With true matinée-idol good looks, Granville-Barker began his stage career as an actor. His early appearances in some of William Poel's Elizabethan Stage Society productions, which emphasized historical accuracy and fidelity to Renaissance stage conventions, proved greatly influential in his later career as a director of Shakespeare. As the lead actor in and director of a number of the premieres of Shaw's works, too—including those in which his wife Lillah McCarthy was cast—he quickly rose to pre-eminence on the Edwardian stage. But it was as a playwright that he became a figure embroiled in controversy. The Lord Chamberlain's Office refused to license his 1907 drama, *Waste,* which was the first play to turn upon the consequences of a female protagonist's abortion, after a failed affair.

The artist responsible for this sketch of the head-turning playwright in his prime was the New York-born Jane Emmet, one of Henry James's cousins by marriage. An accomplished painter, she was also the wife of another artist, the British landscapist Wilfrid de Glehn (1870–1951). Together they formed part of the circle of artistic friends around J.S. Sargent, who painted her on several occasions.

Jane Emmet de Glehn, *Harley Granville-Barker,* pencil, 1912.

Miss Miriam Clements, Mr. Lyn Harding, and Miss Muriel Beaumont in "The Admirable Crichton."
Postcard photograph by. Ellis and Walery, J. Beagles, London, [1908].

In the 1890s, Rudyard Kipling popularized the notion that the real work of "civilizing" throughout the British Empire was being accomplished not by upper-class men, who seemed to him to have become feminized and ineffectual, but by England's "Tommies"—common foot-soldiers drawn from the working classes. In 1902, J.M. Barrie brought a similar perspective to theatrical audiences, arguing in *The Admirable Crichton* that energy and leadership no longer distinguished the deracinated male aristocracy. Instead, these manly qualities could be found in representatives from the servant classes, such as the butler Crichton, who becomes the "natural" ruler of the island on which he and his upper-class employers are stranded by a shipwreck. Yet Barrie added a feminist twist to Kipling's social philosophy, suggesting that upper-class women, too, had the potential for physical prowess, boldness, adventurousness, and appreciation of a challenge lacking in their male counterparts. Shown here is a postcard photograph advertising the second London production of Barrie's play, which was revived in 1908 at the Duke of York's Theatre. It depicts a scene of life on the tropical island, where the erstwhile servant now holds sway and the formerly leisured ladies happily serve and dine with him.

MARK SAMUELS LASNER COLLECTION

Program for *The Admirable Crichton*
by J.M. Barrie.
produced at the Duke of York's Theatre, [1902].

In his 1910 comic one-acter, *The Twelve-Pound Look,* J.M. Barrie would cast a cold eye on what passed for ideals of masculine achievement among the British upper classes. That play, which first bore the ironic title *Success,* would indict fat and complacent business tycoons who lusted after titles and relegated their wives to the status of ornaments, while it praised a feisty divorcée who escaped her materialistic husband and recaptured her integrity by earning her living with a £12 "typing-machine."

Barrie's earlier meditation on the decline of aristocratic masculinity and the growing restlessness of leisured women came in his 1902 comedy, *The Admirable Crichton*. Using pseudo-Darwinian notions of evolutionary fitness and survival, the play dared to suggest that ruling-class Englishmen had degenerated into effete and passive physical specimens; the real energy for Empire-building and innovation was now to be found among working-class men and among women. Despite its unflattering portraits of the very people likely to buy theatre tickets, *The Admirable Crichton* was a tremendous hit when it opened at the Duke of York's Theatre, produced by the American theatrical entrepreneur, Charles Frohman. In the role of Ernest was Gerald du Maurier (1871–1934)—son of the *Punch* artist, George du Maurier (1834–96), whose caricatures of Wilde and other "effeminate" aesthetes had inspired Gilbert and Sullivan's *Patience* a generation before.

Daniel S. O'Connor, ed.
Peter Pan Keepsake. With a Foreword by W. T. Stead.
London: Chatto and Windus, 1907.

As more than one biographer of the popular Scottish playwright has concluded uneasily, J.M. Barrie was something of a "Lost Boy" himself, with a deep attraction to other such "Boys." It was hardly surprising that, despite the respect for powerful women which he professed through numerous stage works, his own marriage should have failed. (His unhappy partner was the actress Mary Ansell who, years before her marriage, allegedly had enjoyed a flirtation with another connoisseur of female performers, the poet and critic Arthur Symons.) After this ill-fated foray in conventional domesticity, Barrie instead strengthened his romantic devotion to an entire family, that of Sylvia and Arthur Llewelyn Davies. Sylvia (1866–1910), a theatrical dressmaker who sewed costumes for Ellen Terry until her marriage, was also the daughter of George du Maurier and younger sister to Gerald du Maurier, who would star in Barrie's *The Admirable Crichton* (1902) and *What Every Woman Knows* (1908). Gerald du Maurier's greatest acclaim, however, resulted from his doubling of the roles of the patriarchal Mr. Darling and the piratical Captain Hook in Barrie's immensely successful *Peter Pan,* which debuted on 27 December 1904 at the Duke of York's Theatre.

Barrie's creation of this fantasy was prompted by his writing of an earlier Christmas pantomime (*The Greedy Dwarf*) for the amusement of the Llewelyn Davies children. But it was clear that *Peter Pan* reached deeper into the playwright's own psyche and also touched secret recesses in the Edwardian audiences who flocked to it. With its gender confusion, its promise of escape to a "Never-Never-Never-Land" free of adult responsibilities, its proud flouting of the laws of time, space, and gravity, and its sentimental ideal of maternal care, *Peter Pan* became the perfect expression for its day of rebellion, nostalgia, and sexual emotions too complex and too outré to be named. The *Peter Pan* craze inspired a variety of theatrical souvenirs, such as this "keepsake" book with photographic illustrations featuring Hilda Trevelyan in the title role.

16

Daniel S. O'Connor, ed., *Peter Pan Keepsake*, 1907.

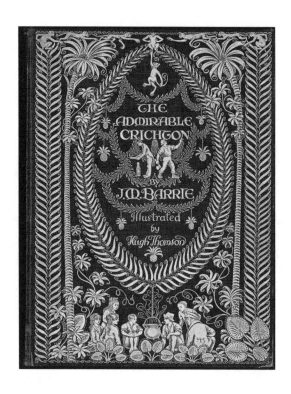

J.M. [James Matthew] Barrie
The Admirable Crichton. Illustrated by Hugh Thomson.
London: Hodder and Stoughton, [1914].

Just as the Irish outsiders Wilde and Shaw had dedicated themselves to laughing at every one of English society's sacred cows, from marriage to business to Parliament, so J.M. Barrie (1860–1937), a Scotsman, specialized in mocking the institutions and hierarchies that England held dear. These included gender hierarchies. Through a succession of plays, including *What Every Woman Knows* (1908), he championed the wisdom and strength of women. At the same time, his comedies (unlike Wilde's or Shaw's) showed just enough respect for marriage as a high ideal, in need of reform but not of dismantling, to appeal even to conservative audiences. The result was widespread financial success for Barrie's works, which could earn money not only on the stage but in book form. Clearly, the publishing firm of Hodder and Stoughton saw the text of *The Admirable Crichton* as a potential source of profit twelve years after the play's first production onstage. It received the "deluxe" treatment in this edition, with full-color illustrations by the artist Hugh Thomson and a red cloth binding that featured a fanciful gilt design depicting the palm trees and monkeys on the tropical island where the play's characters are stranded.

Max Beerbohm
George Bernard Shaw.
Pencil, ink, and wash, [1907].

It is possible that this vision of G. B. Shaw (1856–1960) by Max Beerbohm was inspired by a performance of the "Don Juan in Hell" section of *Man and Superman* at
London's Royal Court Theatre in the year 1907. It is equally possible that it served
as a witty allusion to the title of Shaw's *The Devil's Disciple* (1900), which J. E.
Vedrenne and Harley Granville-Barker also produced at the Savoy Theatre in 1907.
But then again, it is just as likely that this caricature of Shaw with diabolical horns
and a sinuous, reptilian tail represented Beerbohm's view in general of the playwright—a man, as Charles Dickens's Major Joe Bagstock might have said, who was
"tough, and de-vilish sly!"

MARK SAMUELS LASNER COLLECTION

[121]

George Bernard Shaw

Press Cuttings: A Topical Sketch. Compiled from the Editorial and Correspondence Columns of the Daily Papers, as Performed by the Civic and Dramatic Guild at the Royal Theatre, London, on the 9th July, 1909.
London, Constable, 1909.

Long before he turned to writing for the theatre himself, G. B. Shaw saw plays used to great effect as political vehicles by his friends and comrades in the British socialist movement of the 1880s. He was present, for instance, at the October 1887 production by the Socialist League at its office in the Farringdon Road of *The Tables Turned, or Nupkins Awakened*. Commenting afterwards on this short comedy with a pro-proletarian agenda by his early hero, the designer and poet William Morris (1834–1896), Shaw remarked that he had never seen any stage work have a more successful first night. The lessons he learned in the Socialist League remained with him later in life, for he turned repeatedly to what we now would call "agitprop," creating plays (especially shorter ones) meant to entertain the already converted and to enlist the unconverted in support of a particular cause. An avowed feminist and a vocal proponent of women's suffrage, Shaw wrote *Press Cuttings* in 1909 for just such a dual purpose. The copy of *Press Cuttings* shown here is accompanied by the program for its 1911 production by the Bryn Mawr Chapter of the College Equal Suffrage League.

[George Bernard Shaw]
Pygmalion: A Play in Five Acts. By a Fellow of the Royal Society of Literature. Rough Proof—Unpublished.
London: Constable, 1913.

"I washed my face and hands afore I come, I did," announced Eliza Doolittle, as she invaded Professor Henry Higgins's home and speech laboratory in Wimpole Street. But no amount of scrubbing could lessen the shock of her appearance as the female protagonist in a sophisticated drawing-room comedy. Such "draggletailed guttersnipes" as Eliza sometimes turned up in bit parts; often, laced into respectable uniforms, they took the role of maids or other servants in scenes which inevitably focused on characters of a higher class. But they were never the heroines, let alone the romantic leads. And they never, ever spoke the word "bloody"—rather than the less offensive euphemism, "blooming"—on the stage, the way Shaw's forthright heroine did so startlingly.

G. B. Shaw wrote the part of Eliza for Mrs. Patrick Campbell, who was nearly fifty when she starred in *Pygmalion* in 1914. Playing opposite her at the first performance in England (there had been an earlier one in Vienna the year before) on 11 April 1914 at His Majesty's Theatre was Sir Herbert Beerbohm Tree, who had been knighted in 1907. The casting represented a nod to the past—indeed, to Shaw's own past. So, too, did the use of aesthetic-movement set decoration, recalling the look of 1880's interiors, for the drawing-room of Henry Higgins's mother. But the play's characters were new types—not just the indomitable working-class heroine, who both learned from her social "betters" and taught them important lessons, but also the anti-hero-ish hero, Professor Higgins, who combined hyper-masculine bullying with moments of unexpected feminine tenderness and admitted to being something of a spiritual heir to Barrie's "Lost Boys," saying, "I've never been able to feel really grown-up and tremendous, like other chaps."

This is the third in a series of privately printed versions of the play. It was printed for use during rehearsals before the 1914 London opening.

SPECIAL COLLECTIONS DEPARTMENT, UNIVERSITY OF DELAWARE LIBRARY

Claud Lovat Fraser
George Bernard Shaw.
Watercolor, 1911.

If G. B. Shaw looked smug in this watercolor sketch, he had every reason to be (although the self-satisfied attitude long predated his actual accomplishments). In 1911, when Claud Lovat Fraser (1890–1921) dashed off this full-length portrait, Shaw stood—or, as we see here, lounged casually—at the top of the London theatrical scene. Having shucked a critically and financially unrewarding career as a novelist, then a more influential position as the drama critic for *The Saturday Review* from 1895 to 1898 (when he was succeeded there by Max Beerbohm), Shaw found his true calling as a writer for the stage, where he followed Oscar Wilde's path as an Irish dramatist locked in a love-hate relationship with English audiences.

The first of his plays to reach the stage was *Widowers' Houses,* which received a "private," subscribers-only production by the Independent Theatre; the first in a public performance was *Arms and the Man,* which Florence Farr brought to the Avenue Theatre in 1894, as part of the same season in which she also produced Yeats's *The Land of Heart's Desire.* Indeed, one way or another, Shaw owed much of his early success to women, whether as actresses, producers, or financiers of his work, and he paid the debt through his feminist and pro-suffrage pronouncements, as well as his consistent representation of women onstage as figures of ambition and intelligence. His interest in the "Woman Question" and his creation of appealing parts for female leads—in plays ranging from *Candida* and *Major Barbara* to *Caesar and Cleopatra*—continued throughout the first two decades of the twentieth century, even after his popularity began to owe more to the efforts of male actors and directors, such as Harley Granville-Barker and J. E. Vedrenne.

Claud Lovat Fraser, *George Bernard Shaw,* watercolor, 1911.

Gladys Cooper, postcard photograph, [1917].

Gladys Cooper.
Postcard photograph by Rotary Photographic Co., London, [1917].

Gladys Cooper (1888–1971), who was not yet born when the Savoy Theatre turned on its electric lights for the first time in 1881, represented a new generation of London stage performers. Hers was a generation that came of age after the Wilde trials, after the introduction of Ibsen to England, after the heyday of the "New Woman," and after the controversies over the "immorality" of the music halls. Unlike female predecessors such as Elizabeth Robins, who had struggled against the domination of the theatre by a handful of male actor-managers, Cooper entered a more fluid theatrical world. Thus, she could move more easily into management herself, which she did early in her career, taking over the Playhouse Theatre in 1916 with Frank Curzon as her partner and later assuming sole control of it. At that theatre, which in 1894 had been the site of Florence Farr's production of *Arms and the Man* by G.B. Shaw, Cooper staged many new works. But one of her greatest successes was a 1922 revival of Pinero's "problem play" about the "fallen woman," *The Second Mrs. Tanqueray*, in which she played the role that had made a star of Mrs. Patrick Campbell.

Despite positive advances in the lives of women and of actresses, however, this publicity postcard dating from World War I also suggests how little some things had changed since the 1880s. Gladys Cooper may appear here with bobbed hair (the sign of modernity and independence), but she is posed nonetheless with a sprig of flowers, the traditional emblem of "blossoming" femininity and sexual passivity. Her initial popularity, moreover, owed much to her willingness to be photographed in such glamour shots, which marketed her not as an artist or a stage professional, but as a "classic English beauty," much as Lillie Langtry had been marketed some forty years before.

MARK SAMUELS LASNER COLLECTION

Grace Crawford as a Faun.
Photograph, [1916].

All throughout the period from 1880 to 1920, the London stage was a place of cultural cross-fertilization and exchange, energized by what it imported from Ireland, France, the United States, and Norway. In 1911, Covent Garden saw the arrival of a new and potent influence with the first London performances by "Les Ballets Russes de Diaghilev." Over the next few years, the androgynous figure of Nijinsky, which combined "masculine" power with "feminine" grace, and the revolutionary ideas in costuming and set design of Léon Bakst would have a tremendous impact upon British theatre professionals, as well as upon audiences. The Russian ballet inspired Hugo Rumbold, a British stage designer, to join with the conductor Thomas Beecham in creating their own version of Debussy's *L'après-midi d'un Faune* as a mime-play, which went into rehearsals at the Lyric Theatre in August 1916 (although the photograph shown here suggests that it was also performed as an outdoor entertainment for a few invited guests.)

Grace Crawford, the production's cross-dressed (or perhaps cross-species-dressed) Faun, was born in America to a prominent yet often impecunious family, spent her early years at the turn of the century traveling across Europe with her mother, and led a life that was at once respectable and bohemian. At the age of fourteen, she became friends with Stella Patrick Campbell, the daughter of Mrs. Patrick Campbell and later a successful actress herself. When she was fifteen, Crawford's parents enrolled her in ballet school, and they offered no resistance to her desire for a career onstage. (Her earliest appearances were as an entertainer for German troops during World War I.) The role in *L'après-midi d'un Faun* proved momentous in her life, for while in the midst of a costume fitting for it, she met Claud Lovat Fraser (1890–1921), who introduced himself by bending down next to her legs and painting the outline of muscles on her tights. They married not long afterwards. Soon, too, Lovat Fraser, an artist who had once studied with Walter Sickert, finished the War service that ruined his health and became an important and innovative stage designer, working with Nigel Playfair at the Lyric Theatre.

CLAUD LOVAT FRASER PAPERS, SEYMOUR ADELMAN COLLECTION, BRYN MAWR COLLEGE LIBRARY

[128]

Grace Crawford as a Faun, photograph, [1916].

ÆSTHETIC LADY and WOMAN OF FASHION"

A drawing by Du Maurier which
appeared in "Punch," April 9th, 1881

Reproduced by permission of the Proprietors of "Punch"

Max Beerbohm, *A Note on "Patience,"* [1919].

Max Beerbohm
A Note on "Patience."
London: J. Miles, [1919].

A new era in British stage history began in October 1881 with the production of *Patience* at the Savoy Theatre—an era that would see the theatrical sphere illuminated by electricity, but also illumined by the light of progressive ideas and social change, particularly where gender was concerned. Much was different in the theatre and in the larger world by the time of this revival of Gilbert and Sullivan's operetta, which ran from November 1919 to January 1920. Unlike their predecessors in 1881, the actresses who appeared in this production had the right to keep and manage their own money, even if they were married. Some of them also had political representation, for in 1918 Parliament granted women over thirty the right to vote—a direct result of the First World War, which made women's contributions as workers newly visible and valued, but also of the long struggle for suffrage carried out simultaneously on the public stage and the theatrical stage by feminist performers and playwrights.

The passage of time could be measured through this revival in other ways. Rupert D'Oyly Carte, who in 1913 took over the D'Oyly Carte Opera Company founded by his late father, now oversaw the production. And in the *Note on "Patience"* which he contributed to the revival, Max Beerbohm made clear the retrospective character of the whole enterprise: "For us moderns, in an age when everything changes so swiftly, there is ever a peculiar fascination in looking back at the immediate past—that period which is so romantic already in its utter remoteness from us." The souvenir booklet, too, linked *Patience* with the past by reproducing an old George du Maurier cartoon satirizing women affiliated with the late-Victorian aesthetic movement.

Yet *Patience* was still relevant in 1920, especially with its ridicule of the stylized self-presentation of "effeminate" male aesthetes. Noël Coward, a new and important inheritor of Oscar Wilde's mantle (or at least of his silk dressing gowns), was already on the scene and soon would dominate the stage as Wilde had done.

MARK SAMUELS LASNER COLLECTION

Max Beerbohm
Mr. Noël Coward.
Proof of the caricature published in *Heroes and Heroines of Bitter Sweet.* [London: Leadlay News Service, 1931].
Color lithograph, [1931].

At the close of the nineteenth century, stage comedy and musical comedy were dominated by the vision of men—playwrights such as Oscar Wilde and W. S. Gilbert and composers such as Sir Arthur Sullivan. Decades later, in the post-World War I era of British theatre, women still were admired largely as comic players and singers, while new generations of men once again were hailed as the important creative figures in theatrical humor.

A writer of peerlessly witty drawing-room dialogue and also a lyricist and composer, Noël Coward (1899–1973) began his long reign over the London theatre in the 1920s. He often appeared in his own plays, using the stage training he received in his youth, when he performed in productions of Barrie's *Peter Pan* and Thomas's *Charley's Aunt.* Both in the construction of his comic one-liners and in his stylized dress and manner, on and off the stage, he was the direct descendant of Oscar Wilde. The degree of Coward's debt to Wilde may be gauged by the ferocity with which he always denied it, even to himself. As late as 1962, he recorded in his diaries that Wilde "was one of the silliest, most conceited and unattractive characters that ever existed. . . . It is extraordinary indeed that such a posing, artificial old queen should have written one of the greatest comedies in the English language." From Wilde's example, nonetheless, Coward learned not only how to challenge British middle-class morality while leaving audiences laughing, but how to manage his own life as a gay man without being prosecuted or persecuted, as Wilde had been.

Max Beerbohm alluded to Coward's gender-bending persona in a 1931 caricature, giving his subject an exaggeratedly feminine hour-glass silhouette. Indeed, the wasp-waisted coat over slim legs made Coward look suspiciously like a turn-of-the-century leading lady. This image was part of a suite of drawings done by Beerbohm for the Leadlay News Service, a London theatrical news agency, to commemorate and capitalize upon the success of Coward's 1929 operetta, *Bitter Sweet.* Among these published caricatures was one of the impresario Charles Blake Cochran (1872–1951), who brought several of Coward's works to the stage and who once had been a schoolmate of Aubrey Beardsley, the "decadent" 1890s artist associated with Beerbohm and Wilde.

MARK SAMUELS LASNER COLLECTION

Max Beerbohm, *Mr. Noel Coward,* proof color lithograph, [1931].

Bibliography

Arliss, George. *Up the Years from Bloomsbury: An Autobiography.* Boston: Little, Brown, 1927.

Beckson, Karl, ed. *The Memoirs of Arthur Symons: Life and Art in the 1890s.* University Park, PA, and London: Pennsylvania State University Press, 1977.

Beckson, Karl. *The Oscar Wilde Encyclopedia.* New York: AMS Press, 1998.

Beerbohm, Max. "A Defence of Cosmetics." *The Yellow Book: An Illustrated Quarterly.* Vol I (April 1894): 65–82.

Birkin, Andrew. *J. M. Barrie and the Lost Boys.* London: Constable, 1979.

Bradley, Ian. *The Complete Annotated Gilbert and Sullivan.* Oxford: Oxford University Press, 1996.

Chothia, Jean, ed. *The New Woman and Other Emancipated Woman Plays.* Oxford and New York: Oxford University Press, 1998.

Foulkes, Richard, ed. *British Theatre in the 1890s: Essays on Drama and the Stage.* Cambridge: Cambridge University Press, 1992.

Frazier, Adrian. *George Moore, 1852–1933.* New Haven and London: Yale University Press, 2000.

Fraser, Grace Lovat. *In the Days of My Youth.* London: Cassell, 1970.

Gardner, Vivien and Susan Rutherford, eds. *The New Woman and Her Sisters: Feminism and Theatre, 1850–1914.* Ann Arbor: University of Michigan Press, 1992.

Grossmith, George and Weedon. *The Diary of a Nobody.* 1892. rpt. Harmondsworth, Middlesex: Penguin, 1977.

Gwynn, Stephen. "Memoir." *Letters from a Field Hospital* by Mabel Dearmer. London: Macmillan, 1915, 1–73.

Harland, Henry. "I–Mercedes." "Two Sketches." *The Yellow Book: An Illustrated Quarterly.* Vol I (April 1894): 135–42.

Hartnoll, Phyllis. *The Oxford Companion to the Theatre.* 4th ed. Oxford: Oxford University Press, 1983.

Hoare, Philip. *Oscar Wilde's Last Stand: Decadence, Conspiracy, and the Most Outrageous Trial of the Century.* New York, Arcade: 1998.

Holledge, Julie. *Innocent Flowers: Women in Edwardian Theatre.* London: Virago, 1981.

Kaplan, Joel H. and Sheila Stowell. *Theatre and Fashion: Oscar Wilde to the Suffragettes.* Cambridge: Cambridge University Press, 1994.

Merrick, Leonard. *The Actor-Manager.* London: Grant Richards, 1898.

Moore, George. "Is the Theatre a Place of Amusement?" *Beltaine: The Organ of the Irish Literary Theatre.* No. 2 (February 1900): 7–10.

——. *A Mummer's Wife: A Realistic Novel.* London: Vizetelly & Co., 1885.

Moore, Sturge T. and D. C. eds. *Works and Days from the Journal of Michael Field.* London: John Murray, 1933.

Morgan, Fidelis, ed. *The Years Between: Plays by Women on the London Stage, 1900–1950.* London: Virago, 1994.

Mullin, Donald. *Victorian Actors and Actresses in Review: A Dictionary of Contemporary Views of Representative British and American Actors and Actresses, 1837–1901*. Westport, CT: Greenwood Press, 1983.

Nelson, Alfred L. and Gilbert B. Cross. *The Adelphi Theatre, 1806–1900*. http//www.emich.edu/public/english/adelphi_calendar/hst.

Nicoll, Allardyce. *A History of English Drama, 1660–1900*. Cambridge: Cambridge University Press, 1967.

Paston, George [Emily Morse Symonds]. *A Writer of Books*. 1898. rpt. Chicago: Academy Chicago, 1999.

Payn, Graham and Sheridan Morley, eds. *The Noël Coward Diaries*. Boston and Toronto: Little, Brown, 1982.

Powell, Kerry. *Oscar Wilde and the Theatre of the 1890s*. Cambridge: Cambridge University Press, 1990.

Scotson-Clark, G. F. *The "Halls."* London: T. Fisher Unwin, 1899.

Shaw, [George] Bernard. *Arms and the Man*. *Bernard Shaw: Selected Plays with Prefaces*. Vol. 3. New York: Dodd Mead, [n. d.], 123–96.

——. *Mrs. Warren's Profession*. *Bernard Shaw: Selected Plays with Prefaces*. Vol. 3. New York: Dodd Mead, [n. d.], 1–122.

Sloan, John. *Oscar Wilde*. Oxford: Oxford University Press, 2003.

Spender, Dale and Carole Hayman, eds. *How the Vote Was Won and Other Suffragette Plays*. London and New York: Methuen, 1985.

Stowell, Sheila. *A Stage of Their Own: Feminist Playwrights of the Suffrage Era*. Manchester: Manchester University Press, 1992.

Symons, Arthur. *London Nights*. London: Leonard C. Smithers, 1895.

——. *Arthur Symons: Selected Letters, 1880–1935*. Eds. Karl Beckson and John M. Munro. Iowa City: University of Iowa Press, 1989.

Wilde, Oscar. *An Ideal Husband*. *The Picture of Dorian Gray and Other Writings*. Ed. Richard Ellmann. Toronto and New York: 1982, 297–396.

Woodfield, James. *English Theatre in Transition, 1881–1914*. London and Sydney: Croom Helm and Totowa, NJ: Barnes & Noble, 1984.

Index